INTELLECTUAL MOVEMENTS
IN MODERN
EUROPEAN HISTORY

MAIN THEMES IN EUROPEAN HISTORY

Bruce Mazlish, General Editor

EXPLORATION AND DISCOVERY
edited by Robert Albion

EUROPEAN SOCIAL CLASS: STABILITY AND CHANGE
edited by Bernard Barber and Elinor G. Barber

INTELLECTUAL MOVEMENTS IN MODERN
EUROPEAN HISTORY
edited by Franklin L. Baumer

THE ROLE OF RELIGION IN MODERN
EUROPEAN HISTORY
edited by Sidney A. Burrell

THE DEVELOPMENT OF WESTERN TECHNOLOGY
SINCE 1500
edited by Thomas Parke Hughes

THE DEVELOPMENT OF THE MODERN STATE
edited by Heinz Lubasz

THE RISE OF SCIENCE IN RELATION TO SOCIETY
edited by Leonard M. Marsak

POPULATION MOVEMENTS IN MODERN
EUROPEAN HISTORY
edited by Herbert Moller

IMPERIALISM AND COLONIALISM
edited by George H. Nadel and Perry Curtis

Other volumes in preparation

INTELLECTUAL
MOVEMENTS
IN MODERN
EUROPEAN HISTORY

Edited by

FRANKLIN L. BAUMER
Yale University

THE MACMILLAN COMPANY, NEW YORK
COLLIER-MACMILLAN LIMITED, LONDON

For Constance and Joanna

Library of Congress catalog card number: 65–10960

The Macmillan Company, New York
Collier-Macmillan Canada, Ltd., Toronto, Ontario

Second Printing, 1965

Printed in the United States of America

FOREWORD

History, we are frequently told, is a seamless web. However, by isolating and studying the strands that compose the tapestry of man's past, we are able to discern the pattern, or patterns, of which it is comprised. Such an effort does not preclude a grasp of the warp and woof, and the interplay of the strands; rather, it eventually demands and facilitates such a comprehension. It is with this in mind that the individual volumes of the MAIN THEMES series have been conceived.

The student will discover, for example, that the population changes discussed in one volume relate to the changes in technology traced in another volume; that both changes are affected by, and affect in turn, religious and intellectual developments; and that all of these changes and many more ramify into a complicated historical network through all the volumes. In following through this complex interrelationship of parts, the student recreates for himself the unity of history.

Each volume achieves its purpose, and its appeal to a general audience, by presenting the best articles by experts in the field of history and allied disciplines. In a number of cases, the articles have been translated into English for the first time. The individual volume editor has linked these contributions into an integrated account of his theme, and supplied a selected bibliography by means of footnotes for the student who wishes to pursue the topic further. The introduction is an original treatment of the problems in the particular field. It provides continuity and background for the articles, points out gaps in the existing literature, offers new interpretations, and suggests further research.

The volumes in this series afford the student of history an unusual opportunity to explore subjects either not treated, or touched upon lightly in a survey text. Some examples are population—the dramatis personae of history; war—the way of waging peace by other means; the rise of technology and science in relation to society; the role of

religious and cultural ideas and institutions; the continuous ebb and
flow of exploration and colonialism; and the political and economic
works contrived by modern man. Holding fast to these Ariadne threads,
the student penetrates the fascinating labyrinth of history.

BRUCE MAZLISH
General Editor

CONTENTS

INTRODUCTION

This volume comprises an introduction and ten essays, all by well-known authors, most of which are being reprinted for the first time. While there is no single theme running through the essays, they have a common motif. Each deals with a major intellectual movement or "revolution" in "modern" European history. Naturally, a larger volume would have made possible the inclusion of still other important movements: for instance, Liberalism, Positivism, and Historicism. Yet no one will deny that the movements here represented are major: major in the sense that they have profoundly altered Western ways of thinking and thus helped to shape the modern mind.

Two of the terms used in the title—"movement," in the sense of "revolution," and "modern"—require a word of explanation. To most people the term "revolution" probably still connotes a cataclysm or sharp break with the past. The tendency in recent historiography, however, has been to play down this cataclysmic aspect and to emphasize continuity. "Intellectual revolutions," observes one historian, "are like political revolutions, only more so, political revolutions tending to vanish under the cold eye of the historian, until the new régime is only the legalization and continuation of a movement begun in the old, and intellectual revolutions often reducing themselves to little more than the synthesizing and popularizing of ideas long current." [1] These two views are not, I think, mutually exclusive. Clearly, intellectual revolutions do not break out suddenly, like Athena from the head of Zeus. The Darwinian Revolution, for example, would be inexplicable without a long chain of Revolutionary thinking extending back at least to the eighteenth century. On the other hand, intellectual revolutions, regardless of their antecedents, do touch off important changes in thinking. Perhaps we might say of them, then, that they are evolutionary in their origins and early development, revolutionary in their effects. All the essays in this volume assume this double aspect of revolution

[1] Gertrude Himmelfarb, *Darwin and the Darwinian Revolution* (London: Chatto & Windus, 1959), p. 369.

I

even when their main preoccupation is with the "revolutionary" aspect.

The term "modern" also begs definition. In common parlance it may mean simply "present" or "recent," or it may refer to a longer period of time encompassing not only the present but also a considerable segment of the past. Thus, when we speak of "modern art," we may mean art since Matisse or art since Masaccio or even Giotto. In either case, however, the term obviously carries something more than a mere temporal designation. It also implies certain unique characteristics—ideas and attitudes—which supposedly distinguish the "modern" from other types of mind. What are those characteristics? It is with this question in mind that the editor has inserted, early in the argument, a brief discussion by Ernst Troeltsch on "The Meaning of the Modern World." If Troeltsch's discussion, penned in 1911, now seems a bit old-fashioned, it has the merit at least of bringing the problem to the fore. Troeltsch, of course, thought of "modern" as an antonym for "medieval," just as others before him—for instance, the self-styled "Moderns" of the seventeenth and early eighteenth centuries—had thought of themselves as in opposition (at least in certain fields of knowledge) to the "Ancients." He listed among the chief marks of modernity scientific rationalism, individualism, and relativism. Denizens of a more recent "Modern World," we may doubt how well these terms apply to minds shaken by "the death of God," depth psychology, and various forms of collectivism. This is not the place to try to settle this problem. The purpose here is merely to raise the question of definition (what is "modern"?) in what follows, and hopefully to persuade the reader to work out a definition for himself—as indeed he must, for it is not easy to reconcile under one general rubric the "isms" represented in this volume.

Had space permitted it would have been useful to lead off with a prefatory essay dealing not only with these problems, but also with the many other problems encountered in the study of intellectual history. For intellectual history (sometimes called the history of ideas, and sometimes the sociology of knowledge) is a tricky subject, more beset by difficulties, more speculative in certain respects, than any other kind of history. In lieu of such an essay the reader is urged to consult discussions of the general subject, printed elsewhere, by Arthur Lovejoy, Karl Mannheim, and others.[2] If not essential to the essays that follow, these

[2] See especially Arthur O. Lovejoy, "Reflections on the History of Ideas," *Journal of the History of Ideas,* Jan. 1940, pp. 3–23; Karl Mannheim, *Essays on the Sociology of Culture* (London: Routledge & Paul, 1956); Crane Brinton,

discussions will certainly illuminate them. For inevitably most of the latter touch on one or more of the major problems of intellectual history at some point. Lovejoy's essay on Romanticism, for instance, poses the "climate of opinion" problem, as does Rollo May in the parallel he attempts to draw between existentialism and depth psychology in the twentieth century. Troeltsch, as has been said, grapples with the problem of periodization, and both he and Henri Peyre study the nexus between ideas and events. Basil Willey and Lovejoy, among others, deal with the migration of ideas from one realm of thought to others for which they were not originally intended, and so on.

Implicit in all these essays is a distinction, which should be made clear at the outset, between intellectual history and the history of philosophy. Intellectual history cuts the wider swath and has a different purpose. It is concerned centrally with what Professor Cornford calls "the unwritten philosophy" which expresses itself not only in formal philosophy but also in other realms of thought. "If we look beneath the surface of philosophical discussion," Cornford writes, "we find that its source is largely governed by assumptions that are seldom, or never mentioned. I mean that groundwork of current conceptions shared by all the men of any given culture and never mentioned because it is taken for granted as obvious." [3] An intellectual revolution occurs when this unwritten philosophy begins to change significantly—that is, when for a variety of historical reasons thinking men in significant numbers begin to ask new questions and to be concerned about new problems. The impetus may come from non-philosophers—a Jesus in the case of the "Christian Revolution," or a Darwin or Freud. Intellectual history also tries, of course, as the history of philosophy does not, to gauge the effect of these new thinking patterns on human behavior and institutions as well as ideas.

The first essay of this collection plunges the reader into that movement or revolution which is called the Renaissance. The Renaissance, of course, has been, and continues to be, one of the most hotly debated subjects of modern historiography. Was the Renaissance a revolution at all? Is it to be regarded primarily as a continuation or waning of

---

Ideas and Men (Englewood Cliffs, N. J.: Prentice-Hall, 1950); and Franklin L. Baumer, "Intellectual History and Its Problems," *Journal of Modern History*, Sept. 1949, pp. 191–203, and *Main Currents of Western Thought* (New York: Alfred A. Knopf, revised ed., 1964).

[3] F. M. Cornford, *The Unwritten Philosophy and Other Essays* (Cambridge: Cambridge University Press, 1950), p. viii.

the Middle Ages, or as the beginning of the Modern Age? Was it essentially pagan or Christian?

Although the interpretations differ, no one questions that the Renaissance was bound up with something called humanism, and that humanism centered in, among other things, a "philosophy of man." Professor Kristeller's essay has the merit (1) of clearly defining Renaissance humanism, and (2) of disentangling humanism from the other two great currents of early Italian Renaissance thought, Platonism and Aristotelianism. Despite important differences among the three— the Platonists and Aristotelians were obviously more philosophical and systematic, and the Aristotelians were more secular—Kristeller nevertheless detects in their thought a mutual interest. All had in common a preoccupation with man: man's dignity, his special end or purpose, his capacities and powers. This "philosophy of man" was, as Cornford would say, the unwritten philosophy, the "groundwork of current conceptions" shared by the majority of the intellectuals of the early Italian Renaissance.

But was it new? It was not new if by "new" is meant a lack of medieval (or antique) antecedents. As Kristeller points out, the glorification of man was not a new discovery of the Renaissance. What was new then, at least in relation to the Middle Ages, was the emphasis. In the Renaissance the emphasis on man "becomes more persistent, and more exclusive." The later Renaissance became increasingly interested in "nature"—that is, science and the philosophy of science. The early Renaissance, however, concerned itself more exclusively with man and his dignity. And this was its main bequest to what we call the modern world. Inspired by antique examples, it established guidelines for the great humanist tradition which, despite frequent assaults upon it, has persisted to the present.

With respect to the essay by Troeltsch we may well ask the same question: Was the Protestant Reformation a revolution? In any case, was it an *intellectual* revolution? Professor Harbison's recent characterization of the Reformation as a "scholar's revolution" sheds new light on the latter question. "In its origins," he reminds us, "the Reformation was a learned movement, an academic affair, a scandal in a university, begun by a professor and spread by his colleagues and students." [4] Troeltsch's essay similarly provides an answer, though not necessarily the only answer, to the more general question.

[4] E. Harris Harbison, *The Christian Scholar in the Age of the Reformation* (New York: Charles Scribner's Sons, 1956), p. 112.

The work of a well-known church historian and leader of the liberal Protestant movement in Germany, this essay created something of a sensation when it first appeared. If its thesis, really a double thesis, has not gone unchallenged, it is still one to be conjured with; indeed, it has come to be thought of as a landmark in Reformation interpretation, comparable in influence to Jacob Burckhardt's "essay" on the Renaissance.[5] Briefly, Troeltsch contended that the Reformation initiated by Luther and Calvin was not intentionally a revolution, but was such only unconsciously and accidentally—that is, in its side-effects. Or to use his own categories, the Reformation belonged more to the Middle Ages than to the Modern World, yet it contributed "in spite of that" to the development of modern life and thought. "Protestantism was, in the first place, simply a modification of Catholicism. . . . But this only makes it a more pressing problem how, in spite of all that, Protestantism could play a conspicuous part in the production of the modern world." The essay discusses this problem at some length, describing in broad strokes the contributions of Protestantism to the modern idea of the State, democracy, capitalism, and science. Patently, Troeltsch wrote under the influence of the new evolutionary point of view in historical interpretation which eschewed sharp breaks in history and stressed continuity with modification.

Since Troeltsch's time it has become quite common to date the beginning of the "Modern World," not with either the Renaissance or Reformation, but with the Scientific Revolution of the sixteenth and seventeenth centuries. The Scientific Revolution, says Herbert Butterfield in a typical statement, "outshines everything since the rise of Christianity and reduces the Renaissance and Reformation to the rank of mere episodes, mere internal replacements, within the system of medieval Christendom."[6] This thesis is debatable, but it is scarcely debatable that the movement led by Copernicus, Galileo, and Newton effected, in Professor Willey's words, "one of the greatest changes which have ever taken place in men's ways of thinking about the world they live in." Two essays, one by Leonardo Olschki, the other by Basil Willey, describe the nature of this change, the first directly by an examination of Galileo's ideas, the second indirectly by a consideration of some of its long-range effects on Western thought and imagination.

Professor Olschki's essay goes brilliantly to the heart of the "New

[5] *The Civilization of the Renaissance in Italy* (many editions).
[6] Herbert Butterfield, *The Origins of Modern Science 1300–1800* (New York: The Macmillan Company, 1951), p. viii.

Philosophy" as represented by Galileo, accenting its radical character—that is, its departure from traditional Greek and scholastic ideas of nature. Olschki might have emphasized, as some others have done, Galileo's affinities with older systems of thought and particularly his indebtedness to the Paduan school from which in a sense he descended. But to have done so would be to miss the essential boldness of his conceptions, his "intellectual courage." In the teeth of the still reigning tradition, Galileo, more distinctly than any of his precursors or contemporaries, interpreted nature in a new way, as a book written in mathematical symbols, and as not only infinite in scope but also homogeneous throughout (thus breaking down the "hierarchy of nobility" of the Aristotelian cosmos). He also authored what might be called science's declaration of independence from theology: the famous letter to the Grand Duchess Christina of Tuscany in which he asserted the supremacy of science within its own sphere—that is, in matters pertaining to "physics"—while conceding to the Church supremacy in "supernatural things which are matters of faith."

No wonder the Scientific Revolution had repercussions, not only in Galileo's time, but even more in later generations. Olschki hints at some of these, but Willey's essay makes them explicit. "New philosophy," as John Donne called it, had two quite different and indeed paradoxical effects on Western thinking. It was both settling and unsettling. If it did not at once "call all in doubt"—Willey reminds us that on the whole science remained "pious" in the seventeenth century, that it was thought to reveal God's power as Bible and Church revealed His saving grace—in the long run it unquestionably undermined "traditional religious sentiment." The new naturalism, explaining things by natural, physical causes, made supernaturalism seem supererogatory. The idea of infinity too was disturbing, even to such a deeply religious man as Pascal: "The eternal silence of these infinite spaces frightens me." As Martin Buber would say, the universe could no longer be experienced as a house or home for man to dwell in. "The original contract between the universe and man is dissolved and man finds himself a stranger and solitary in the world." [7] Yet the new science was also, paradoxically, a source of security as well as insecurity, of excitement and even exhilaration. If the new universe, Galileo's world-machine, was comparatively impersonal and mechanistic, it was also rational and predictable. If it made some men feel small, it made others feel big by

[7] Martin Buber, *What is Man?* in *Between Man and Man* (Boston: Beacon Press, 1959), p. 132.

their ability to decipher it more precisely than their forefathers had ever done, and thus to control it for the relief of man's estate. This note on power, so conspicuous in Francis Bacon, leads directly to the revolution known as the Enlightenment.

Professor Peyre's essay does not address itself directly to the much debated question of what the Enlightenment was. He asks a different sort of question: What effect, if any, do ideas have on great political and social events? Specifically, in what relation did the *philosophes* stand to the French Revolution? Inevitably, however, this latter question begs the former, and in fact Peyre not only characterizes the Enlightenment in passing but reviews much of the important historiography of the subject since the time of Hippolyte Taine.

In reply to his main question Peyre affirms—correctly, in my opinion—that professional historians tend to limit too much the role played by ideas in history. Though by no means oblivious of "the purely historical causes," including the economic, he also directs attention to "the slow subterranean movements" which work on men's minds and eventually influence their behavior. The Enlightenment, he thinks, was such a movement. The *philosophes* did not want a revolution; but they prepared the way for revolution, by slowly undermining traditional beliefs, developing a critical spirit, and teaching the idea of progress. "Eighteenth-century philosophy taught the Frenchman to find his condition wretched, or in any case, unjust and illogical, and made him disinclined to the patient resignation to his trouble that that long characterized his ancestors." As Peyre goes on to say, however, logic never fully persuades. Hence, in assessing the power of ideas to foment revolution, one has to take into account, in addition to "logical" ideas, another class of ideas which the French call *"idées-forces."* An *idée-force* is an effective idea—a formula, perhaps, or a quotation torn from its context—which has the power to inflame the passions and incite to action. Thus did Rousseau's "Man is born free, and everywhere he is in chains" powerfully influence Frenchmen throughout the Revolution.

In the next essay, Professor Arthur O. Lovejoy juxtaposes another revolution in ideas—commonly called Romanticism—to the Enlightenment. He emphasizes, quite rightly, the ambiguity of the term "Romanticism" which, like the term "nature," has had attached to it a bewildering variety of meanings. Lovejoy's own logic at this point is not entirely unambiguous, for in the next breath he concedes that there was a "Romantic period," covering roughly the half-century from 1780 to 1830, and dominated by German, as the Enlightenment was dominated

by French, ideas. Among the ideas active during this period was the
new valuation put upon the "infinite"—striving without a terminus
(*Streben ins Unendliche*)—as opposed to the traditional tendency to
think in terms of finites, whether in art, literary style, or human
character and conduct. This "revolt against the finite" manifested itself,
not only in the new "romantic" or "modern" art where it commenced,
but also in metaphysics and religion, and not least in the apotheosis of
"the Will" by Schopenhauer and Nietzsche. Lovejoy devotes the concluding section of his essay to tying in this and certain other ideas
peculiar to the Romantic period with recent developments in political
history. It should be remembered that he was writing in 1940 when
Fascism was at flood tide. He is far from suggesting a cause-effect
relationship between Romanticism and Fascism. Nevertheless, he believes that long familiarity with romanticist ideas by the educated
public helped to produce the state of mind necessary for the wide
reception of totalitarian ideologies in Italy and Germany. "There is,"
Lovejoy concludes, "a certain specific historical connection between the
intellectual revolution of the Romantic period and the tragic spectacle
of Europe in 1940."

The impact of three subsequent intellectual movements is much
less tenuous. The twentieth-century mind would simply not be what
it is without the towering figures of Marx, Darwin, and Freud. Each
of these three touched off a revolution, the full implications of which
we have perhaps still not appreciated. From each, as Thomas Mann
says of Freud, evolved a "world movement" which "penetrated into
every field of science and every domain of the intellect." Of the three,
only Marx, and not even Marx completely, meets the specifications for
what Professor Acton calls a "world-outlook"—that is, a systematic
account of the world and man's place in it. Darwin rarely ventured
outside the realm of biology, and Freud, though he made occasional
forays into the philosophy of history and even metaphysics, never
claimed to be anything but a physician of the soul. Others, however,
as is so often the way in intellectual history, have appropriated their
ideas and made them the basic components of "world" systems.

Acton's essay represents Marxism as a "non-religious world-outlook."
Using the works of Lenin and several other later commentators as well
as the original gospels of Marx and Engels, it shows, better than any
other essay I have seen, the interconnection between Marxist metaphysics and the Marxist theory of human purpose. The latter (scientific
socialism) is in fact inexplicable without reference to the former (dialec-

tical materialism.). Professor Acton thus corrects a common impression
that Marxism had no "philosophy." No doubt Marxist thought was
activistic, as traditional philosophy—Hegelianism, for instance—was
contemplative. But this is quite a different thing from saying that
Marxism expressed the "negation of philosophy," as has been alleged.
A materialist metaphysic, as opposed to antimetaphysical positivism and
later phenomenalism, is implicit and sometimes quite explicit in Marxist
writings. To be sure, it was a new kind of materialism, dialectical and
"evolutionary" rather than mechanical. It can be readily seen, however,
how it could be made, and in fact was made, to sustain the Marxist
philosophy of history.

A professor of philosophy cannot be blamed for leaving out much
that would be desirable in a more purely historical essay—a discussion,
for example, of the climate in which Marxism arose, of parallels with
contemporary systems of thought, of the influence of the Marxist
world-view on Western intellectuals. Would that there were space for
another essay specifically on this last subject, and with particular reference to the twentieth century. But this is a whole story in itself and
one, incidentally, not yet told, at least in its larger dimensions. The
materials for such a study, however, lie ready at hand, in the life histories and utterances of such well known intellectuals as Arthur
Koestler, Jean-Paul Sartre, and Bertolt Brecht.[8]

Lovejoy's essay on Darwin is one of his earliest and least well
known. It was written, like John Dewey's famous essay on "The
Influence of Darwinism on Philosophy," for the fiftieth anniversary
of The Origin of Species, and it retains some of the flavor of that
time when Darwinism was still very much a cause célèbre. As J. H.
Randall points out in a recent article,[9] Darwinian interpretation has
gone through a number of phases. Lovejoy's essay (which, incidentally,
Randall does not mention) belongs to a phase, just prior to the first
World War, when Darwinism was having a decidedly sobering effect
on students of religion, ethics, and politics. It should be read therefore
with this phase in mind, but it should also be compared with the
subsequent phase, represented by the works of Julian Huxley and Père
Teilhard de Chardin, which interprets "evolution" less pessimistically.

Actually, Lovejoy deals less with evolution than with natural selec-

---

[8] In addition to chapters in biographies and critical studies, there are several
reasonably good general articles on this subject in George B. de Huszar (ed.),
The Intellectuals (Glencoe: The Free Press, 1960).

[9] John Herman Randall, "The Changing Impact of Darwin on Philosophy,"
in Journal of the History of Ideas, Oct.–Dec. 1961, pp. 435–462.

tion. He points out, quite rightly, that there was nothing peculiarly Darwinian about the general notion of evolution or even the transformation of species, that Darwin merely added scientific support to an idea already widely accepted; hence, Lovejoy concludes that "the distinctive influence of Darwin upon modern thought is the influence of the doctrine of natural selection." The diffusion of this "doctrine," he states, tipped the balance in favor of a mechanistic as opposed to a teleological (and religious) explanation of natural occurrences, and, by its depiction of nature as "red in tooth and claw," both undermined traditional ethics and exacerbated late nineteenth-century pessimism.

Is it possible that Lovejoy, despite his penetrating analysis, mistook the real nerve center of the Darwinian Revolution? Was not the idea of evolution after all the real thing, rather than natural selection? "In laying hands upon the sacred ark of absolute permanency," Dewey writes, "in treating the forms that had been regarded as types of fixity and perfection as originating and passing away, the *Origin of Species* introduced a mode of thinking that in the end was bound to transform the logic of knowledge, and hence the treatment of morals, politics, and religion." Actually, Lovejoy would have agreed to everything in this statement except the word "introduced." With respect to the idea of evolution he would have said that Darwinism did not introduce, it only contributed to, a much larger revolution—we might call it the Time Revolution—which, in Dewey's phrase, has transferred interest "from the permanent to the changing."

Of Thomas Mann's essay on Freud it might be said that it is as much about the author as about his subject. It might also be said that it is essentially an encomium, the tribute of one of the great writers of our time to a "great scientist" (it was, in fact, originally delivered as a speech to commemorate Freud's eightieth birthday). It is, however, much more than mere autobiography or rhetoric. Like Lovejoy's essay on Darwin, it testifies to the influence of a major intellectual figure on Western culture at large—particularly in the field of letters and with particular reference to one man of letters. "It would be too much to say that I came to psychoanalysis," says Mann. "It came to me." The essay also suggests rich parallels between Freud the scientist and certain philosophers of the nineteenth century, notably Arthur Schopenhauer, whose works Freud did not know or else came to late, after he had developed his own "system." Thus, Mann hints at a wider revolution in thought, really a revolution in the whole western conception of the nature of man, of which Freudianism was but one expression though a very powerful one. With fine discrimination he finds the heart of this "new anthropology," which challenged "classic" psychology, in Freud's mature essay on "The Anatomy of the Mental Personality." There, more eloquently and succinctly than anywhere else, the "physicianly psychologist" described the plight of the ego, hemmed in by the primitive, irrational id and the supermoral superego. Possibly the man of letters, his head full of the "analytic revelation," romanticized the hard-boiled scientist a bit too much. Yet Mann is by no means the only one who has detected in Freud a strong romantic strain. "To think of him as a Romantic despite his ardent faith in science," says Philip Rieff, "involves no contradiction, for though he insisted on the pre-rational core of human nature, Freud remained a rationalist." [10] And in the end Mann, too, it would seem, thought of Freud as fundamentally a rationalist who strove to make ego be where id once had been.

There is more about the psychoanalytical movement in the final piece in this collection by Rollo May. Dr. May, who is one of the chief protagonists of the new "existential psychology," relates it to Existentialism as Mann related it (primarily) to the "will" philosophy of Schopenhauer.

Existentialism is much too complicated and diverse a movement to encapsulate in a few lines. Nevertheless, it is important to grasp what it is, for not for nothing has it been called "the philosophy of Europe in this century," "a complete revolution in philosophy." Among other things it is a revolt against the abstractness so highly prized in the Western philosophical tradition and in modern scientific thinking. It is perhaps best understood as a psychologizing philosophy since it centers, not in abstract ideas, but in concrete experience—that is, in vital human interests, of concern to every man, such as death and suffering, which, as Kierkegaard would say, shake the foundations. It is also a protest against collectivism and determinism and, indeed, all forms of modern thought which tend to dehumanize and depersonalize the individual. It restores freedom to man, believing him to be neither exclusively "object" or "machine," a bundle of determined drives, but a whole "being" capable of making free decisions. In comparison to traditional humanism, however, Existentialism stresses the anxiety, even the despair, involved in being free. Abraham is anxious precisely because he is free, because he alone—who else?—chooses whether or

[10] Philip Rieff, *Freud: The Mind of the Moralist* (Garden City: Doubleday & Company, 1961), p. 103.

not to kill his son Isaac, and he alone is responsible for the consequences of his choice. At this point Existentialism mirrors "the psychological predicament of contemporary Western man."

Dr. May's essay successfully catches some of these nuances. It also
shows how the Existentialist Revolution has spread, beyond "philosophy,"
to literature and the arts. And it makes the attempt at least, perhaps not
altogether successfully, to sketch in its historical background. This last
is not simply a question of finding "origins" but of relating the whole
movement commencing with Kierkegaard to the "crisis" in modern
thought and civilization.

I can think of no better way to conclude this introduction than to
quote the words of John Stuart Mill in his famous essay on Coleridge:
"Our object is to invite to the study of the original sources, not to supply
the place of such a study." These words might well serve as the motto
of this volume.

FRANKLIN L. BAUMER

Yale University

Note: In the essays that follow the editor has taken considerable
liberties with the authors' footnotes. He has included only those which
he thought would be particularly useful to the general reader, and he
has added a number of his own, chiefly as helps to further study or
supplementary reading. In accordance with this practice, the notes have
been renumbered. The editor's own footnotes are indicated by brackets.

THE PHILOSOPHY OF MAN IN THE
ITALIAN RENAISSANCE *

Paul Oskar Kristeller †

The achievements of the Italian Renaissance in the fine arts, in
poetry and literature, in historiography and political thought, and in
the natural sciences are well known, and they have been brought home

* Reprinted from *Italica*, June 1947, pp. 93–112. Copyright 1947 by *Italica*.
Used by permission of *Italica* and the author.

† Paul Oskar Kristeller is Professor of Philosophy at Columbia University.
His publications include *The Classics and Renaissance Thought* and *The Philosophy of Marsilio Ficino*.

to us in a number of valuable and interesting lectures. The contributions of Renaissance Italy to learning and to philosophy are perhaps less widely understood, if I am not mistaken.[1] To be sure, the group of natural philosophers of the later sixteenth century, which culminated in Giordano Bruno, has attracted some attention, mainly for their influence on the rise of early science.[2] Yet I shall concentrate today on the earlier phases of Renaissance thought, which have been the center of my studies for a number of years, and accordingly, I shall emphasize, not the philosophy of nature, but the philosophy of man. I shall briefly discuss the three major currents which dominated the development of Italian thought between 1350 and 1520: Humanism, Platonism, and Aristotelianism.

In our contemporary discussions, the term "Humanism" has become one of those slogans which through their very vagueness carry an almost universal and irresistible appeal. Every person interested in "human values" or in "human welfare" is nowadays called a "humanist," and there is hardly any person who would not like to be, or pretend to be, a humanist in this sense of the word. I am afraid, if some of you blame me that I lured you here under false pretenses by using the term "humanism" in the title of my lecture, I must plead guilty. For the humanism of the Renaissance was something quite different from present-day humanism. To be sure, Renaissance humanists were also interested in human values, but this was incidental to their major concern, which was the study and imitation of classical, Greek and Latin literature. This classical humanism of the Italian Renaissance was primarily a cultural, literary, and educational movement, and although it had a definite impact upon Renaissance thought, its philosophical ideas can never be completely detached from its literary

[1] [Kristeller himself has contributed a number of substantial studies on this subject, including *Studies in Renaissance Thought and Letters* (Rome: Edizioni di Storia e Letteratura, 1956); and *The Classics and Renaissance Thought* (Cambridge: Harvard University Press, 1955). See also on Renaissance thought in general: Ernst Cassirer (ed.), *The Renaissance Philosophy of Man* (Chicago: University of Chicago Press, 1948); Denys Hay, *The Italian Renaissance in Its Historical Background* (Cambridge: Cambridge University Press, 1961); W. H. Woodward, *Studies in Education during the Age of the Renaissance, 1400–1600* (Cambridge: Cambridge University Press,1906); and Federico Chabod, *Machiavelli and the Renaissance* (Cambridge: Harvard University Press, 1958). Wallace Ferguson, *The Renaissance in Historical Thought* (Boston: Houghton Mifflin, 1948) is indispensable for interpretations of the Renaissance.]

[2] [On the Renaissance and science see the interesting discussion by Dana B. Durand and Hans Baron in *Journal of the History of Ideas*, Jan. 1943, pp. 1–49. For further references see below, page 42, note 1.]

interests. The term "humanism" as applied to the classicist movement of the Renaissance was coined by historians of the nineteenth century, but the terms "humanities" and "humanist" were coined during the Renaissance itself. Already some ancient Roman authors used the term *Studia humanitatis* to ennoble the study of poetry, literature, and history, and this expression was taken up by the scholars of the early Italian Renaissance to stress the human value of the fields of study which they cultivated: grammar, rhetoric, poetry, history, and moral philosophy, in the sense in which these fields were understood at that time. Soon the professional teacher of these subjects came to be called *humanista,* a "humanist," a term which occurred first in documents of the late fifteenth century and became increasingly common during the sixteenth century.

The origin of Italian humanism is usually attributed to Petrarch, who had a few forerunners, to be sure, but according to the common view, no real predecessors. There is no doubt that Petrarch was the first really great figure among the Italian humanists. Yet some of the characteristic interests and tendencies of Italian humanism preceded Petrarch at least by one generation. The origin and rise of Italian humanism, in my opinion, was due to two, or rather three, different factors. One factor was the native Italian tradition of medieval rhetoric, which had been cultivated by teachers and notaries, and handed down as a technique of composing letters, documents, and speeches. The second factor was the so-called medieval humanism, that is, the study of classical Latin poetry and literature, which had flourished in the schools of the twelfth century, especially in France, and to which Italy at that time had made a very limited contribution.[3] Toward the end of the thirteenth century, this study of the Latin classics was introduced into the Italian schools and merged with the native rhetorical tradition that had been of a much more practical nature. Thus the scholarly study of the Latin classics began to develop once the successful imitation of the classical authors, based on their careful study, was considered as the best training for those who wanted to write and to speak well, in prose and in verse, in Latin and in the vernacular. A third factor was added to this development during the latter half of the fourteenth century: the study of classical Greek literature, which had been almost unknown to the Western Middle Ages, but had been cultivated through the centuries in the Byzantine Empire and was now brought to Italy from

[3] [On medieval humanism see Charles H. Haskins, *The Renaissance of the Twelfth Century* (Cambridge: Harvard University Press, 1927).]

the East as a result of intensified political, ecclesiastic, and scholarly contacts.

The fruit of this combination of scholarly interests was the body of humanistic learning which comprised Latin and Greek grammar, eloquence, poetry, history, and moral philosophy. The humanists occupied the chairs of all these fields at the universities, asserted their importance in relation to the other sciences, and obtained almost complete control of the secondary schools in which grammar and rhetoric always had been the core of the curriculum.

The humanists also acquired considerable prestige and power through the places they held in the various professions. For the humanists were not merely free-lance writers, as it is often asserted, and the case of Petrarch is by no means typical. Most of the humanists belonged to one of three professional groups, and sometimes to more than one at the same time: they were teachers at the universities or secondary schools; or they were secretaries of princes or cities; or they were noble or wealthy amateurs who combined their business or political activities with the fashionable intellectual interests of their time. This professional and social place of the humanists easily explains the range and content of their literary production. They edited, translated, and expounded classical Greek and Latin authors, and wrote on matters of grammar and philology; they composed speeches, letters, poems, historical works, and moral treatises. The bulk of this humanistic literature is enormous, and on the whole it is much more interesting than those who have never read it would have us believe. Much, although not all, of this literature is written in Latin, which accounts in part for the scanty interest it has encountered in recent years. The charge that the works of the humanists are studded with classical quotations and with rhetorical phrases is to some extent correct. Yet we must add that the humanists managed to express in this classicist and rhetorical Latin the nuances of their own personal experience and the realities of contemporary life. A Neolatin literature which contains descriptions of tournaments, and of snowball fights in the streets of fifteenth-century Florence, certainly cannot be dismissed as academic, although its means of expression may be less accessible to us than are the paintings of the same period that reflect similar standards of form and content.

Within the framework of Renaissance learning, humanism certainly occupied a very important place. However, it would be quite wrong to assume, as modern scholars often do, that humanism represents the

complete picture of Renaissance science and philosophy, and that it
tended, or even hoped, to expel and to replace all those traditions of
medieval learning that are usually associated with the term "scholasticism." Humanism originated and developed within the limited area
of rhetorical and philological studies. In asserting the claims of their
own field, the humanists were apt to become aggressive toward their
colleagues in other disciplines, but they were quite unable to provide for
those other fields a subject matter capable of replacing the material
furnished by the medieval tradition. Humanism was and remained a
cultural and literary movement bound by its classical and rhetorical
interests. Its influence on other fields, such as natural philosophy,
theology, law, medicine, or mathematics, could be only external and
indirect.

However, this indirect influence was in many respects quite important, especially in the case of philosophical thought with which we
are primarily concerned. The humanistic movement of the Renaissance
provided philosophers with new standards of literary elegance and of
historical criticism, with additional classical source materials, and consequently with many ancient ideas and philosophies which thus came
to be restated and revived or to be combined with other old and new
doctrines. Moreover, although humanism in itself was not committed
to any particular philosophy, it contained in its very program a few
general ideas that were of great importance for Renaissance thought.
One of these ideas was the conception the humanists had of history
and of their own historical position. They believed that classical
antiquity was in most respects a perfect age; that it was succeeded by a
long period of decline, the Dark or Middle Ages; and that it was the
task and destiny of their own age to accomplish a rebirth or renaissance
of classical antiquity, or of its learning, arts, and sciences. The humanists themselves thus helped to shape the concept of the Renaissance
which has been so bitterly criticized by certain modern historians.

Even more important was the emphasis on man which was inherent
in the cultural and educational program of the Renaissance humanists
and which should endear them even to our contemporary "humanists"
(although the latter would show slight sympathy for the educational
ideals of their Renaissance predecessors). When the Renaissance
humanists called their studies the "humanities" or *Studia humanitatis,*
they expressed the claim that these studies contribute to the education
of a desirable human being, and hence are of vital concern for man as
man. Thus they indicated a basic concern for man and his dignity, and

this aspiration became quite explicit in many of their writings. When Petrarch whom we called the first great humanist describes in a famous letter his trip to the peak of Mont Ventoux, he tells us that over-whelmed by the marvelous view, he took Augustine's *Confessions* out of his pocket and opened it at random. He found the following passage: "Men go to admire the heights of mountains, the great floods of the seas, the courses of rivers, the shores of the ocean, and the orbits of the stars, and neglect themselves." "I was stunned," Petrarch continues, "closed the book and was angry at myself since I was still admiring earthly things although I should have learned long ago from pagan philosophers that nothing is admirable but the soul in comparison to which if it is great nothing is great." Petrarch thus expresses his con-viction that man and his soul are the true standard of intellectual importance, but in doing so, he uses the very words of Augustine, the Christian classic, and of Seneca, the pagan classic.

About the middle of the fifteenth century, the Florentine humanist, Giannozzo Manetti, composed a lengthy treatise on the dignity and excellence of man, which was written as a conscious reply to Pope Innocent III's treatise on the miserable condition of mankind. Manetti's work is filled with quotations from Cicero and from Lactantius. Also among later humanists, the dignity of man continued to be a favorite topic. None of them expressed the link between this concern for man and the admiration of antiquity more clearly than the great author who has been called a vernacular humanist. For Machiavelli who in his enforced retirement liked to put on evening clothes to converse with the great ancient writers, the study of ancients was valuable because they were human models, and the attempt to imitate them was not vain since human nature is always the same.

Whereas the humanistic movement had a literary and cultural origin and character and hence had merely an indirect, though power-ful, influence on the development of philosophical thought, the second great intellectual movement of the early Renaissance, Platonism, was philosophical in its origin and had but an incidental, though very significant, impact upon Renaissance literature.[4] Considering the quantity of its literary production and the number of its followers, Platonism was not as broad a current as was humanism, but it was much deeper, both in the wealth of its ideas and in the response it evoked from its adherents. Platonism, to be sure, had its own centers

[4] [On Renaissance Platonism see, in addition to Kristeller's studies, Nesca A. Robb, *Neoplatonism of the Italian Renaissance* (London: Allen & Unwin, 1935).]

in such informal and temporary circles as the Platonic Academy of
Florence, as well as in certain literary Academies of the sixteenth
century and in a few university chairs of Platonic philosophy. Yet
taken as a whole, Platonism did not possess the strong institutional and
professional support which both humanism and Aristotelianism were
enjoying. Platonism owed its influence rather to the personal appeal
of its ideas to the experiences and inclinations of individual thinkers
and writers, an appeal that varied in depth and sincerity and that sometimes, as things go, degenerated into a mere fashion.

The Platonism of the Italian Renaissance as it culminated in
Marsilio Ficino, the leader of the Florentine Academy, and in his friend
and pupil, Giovanni Pico della Mirandola,[5] was in many respects an
offshoot of the humanistic movement. Both Ficino and Pico had enjoyed
a thorough humanistic education and were imbued with the stylistic
and classicist standards of the humanists. Their preference for Plato
had its antecedents in Petrarch and in other early humanists. Ficino's
endeavor to translate and to expound the works of Plato and of the
ancient Neoplatonists was comparable to the work done by the humanists
on other classical authors. His attempt to restate and to revive the
teachings of Platonism reflected the general trend toward reviving
ancient arts, ideas, and institutions, and in one of his letters he compared his own revival of Platonic philosophy to the rebirth of grammar,
poetry, rhetoric, painting, sculpture, architecture, music, and astronomy
which had been accomplished in his century. However, Renaissance
Platonism had other roots outside the traditions and interests of early
humanism. One of these roots was the Aristotelianism or scholasticism
of the later Middle Ages which continued to dominate the teaching
of philosophy at the universities and other schools. We know now
beyond any doubt that Ficino absorbed this kind of training as a student
at the University of Florence, whereas it had never been questioned
that Pico had studied scholastic philosophy at the universities of Padua
and of Paris. This training left profound traces in their thought and
writings. It enabled them to proceed beyond the amateurish and vague
ideas of the earlier humanists to a serious and methodical kind of
philosophical speculation which could have an influence on profes-
sionally trained philosophers and which was taken seriously even by

[5] [The standard book on Ficino in English is Paul Oskar Kristeller, *The
Philosophy of Marsilio Ficino* (New York: Columbia University Press, 1943).
On Pico see Ernst Cassirer's two articles in *Journal of the History of Ideas*, April
and June 1942, pp. 123–144, 319–346.]

their philosophical opponents. Consequently, Ficino and Pico abandoned the superficial polemic of the earlier humanists against scholastic philosophy, and gladly acknowledged their indebtedness to Aristotle and to the medieval thinkers. In an interesting correspondence with Ermolao Barbaro, Pico took up the defense of the medieval philosophers, stressing the point that philosophical content is much more important than literary form. Another source of Renaissance Platonism, which distinguishes it both from humanism and Aristotelianism, was the heritage of medieval mysticism and Augustinianism. Even after the thirteenth century when Aristotelianism had become predominant in the teaching of philosophy and theology, the older current of Augustinianism survived among the Franciscan theologians, and in a vaguer form in the growing popular religious literature which developed around the religious associations for laymen. There are several indications that Ficino was strongly influenced by this brand of religious spiritualism, and Pico's later writings and his relationship to Savonarola show that he had similar inclinations. If we realize that Ficino's Academy resembled in many respects such an association of laymen in which classical scholarship and secular philosophy were added to a basically religious atmosphere, we can better understand the impression which this Academy made upon the educated circles of Medicean Florence, and upon the imagination of later generations.

Due to these additional philosophical and religious resources, Platonism was able to transform some of the vague ideas and aspirations of the early humanists into definite and elaborate speculative theories. Especially did the emphasis on man which had been one of the most characteristic aspirations of early humanist thought receive a more systematic philosophical expression in the works of the Renaissance Platonists.

Ficino's major philosophical work, the *Platonic Theology,* contains several passages in which the excellence and dignity of man is emphasized. Man is superior to other creatures in the variety of his arts and skills. With his thought and with his desire, he passes through all parts of the universe, is related to all of them, and has a share in them all. The human soul is directed both toward God and toward the body, that is both toward the intelligible and toward the corporeal world. Hence it participates both in time and in eternity. These ideas are embodied in Ficino's scheme of a universal hierarchy in which the human soul occupies a privileged, central place: God, the Angelic Mind, the Rational Soul, Quality, and Body. Due to its central position, the soul is able to mediate between the upper and the lower half of reality, between the intelligible and the corporeal. Ficino, who had borrowed many elements of his scheme from Neoplatonic tradition, consciously modified it in this decisive point, the central position of the human soul. "This (the soul) is the greatest of all miracles in nature. All other things beneath God are always one single being, but the soul is all things together. . . . Therefore it may be rightly called the center of nature, the middle term of all things, the series of the world, the face of all, the bond and juncture of the universe."

The same idea is taken up and further developed by Pico in his famous *Oration on the Dignity of Man*. Pico stresses especially man's freedom to choose his way of life. Consequently, man no longer occupies any fixed place in the universal hierarchy, not even the privileged central place, but he is entirely detached from that hierarchy and constitutes a world in himself. Illustrating this conception with a story, Pico recounts that man was created last among all things when God had already distributed all His gifts among the other creatures.

Finally, the Best of Workmen decided that that to which nothing of its very own could be given should be given, in composite fashion, whatsoever had belonged individually to each and every thing . . . and He spoke to him as follows: We have given thee, Adam, no fixed seat, no form of thy very own, no gift peculiarly thine, that . . . thou mayest . . . possess as thine own the seat, the form, the gifts which thou thyself shalt desire. . . . In conformity with thy free judgment in whose hands I have placed thee, thou art confined by no bonds, and thou wilt fix the limits of thy nature for thyself. . . . Neither heavenly nor earthly, neither mortal nor immortal have We made thee. Thou . . . art the moulder and maker of thyself. . . . Thou canst grow downward into the lower natures which are brutes. Thou canst again grow upward from the mind's reason into the higher natures which are divine.

The concern for man and the meaning of his life determines also another basic theory of Ficino, the doctrine of immortality to which he devotes the largest part of his chief philosophical work, the *Platonic Theology*. Ficino does not condemn or minimize the practical activities of life, but he states with great emphasis that the main purpose of human life is contemplation. By contemplation he understands a spiritual experience which begins with a detachment of our mind from the outside world, which then proceeds through various degrees of knowledge and desire, and finally culminates in the immediate vision and enjoyment of God. Since this final union with God is rarely attained during the present life, Ficino postulates a future life in which this aim will be attained in a permanent fashion by all those who made the necessary effort during the present life. The immortality of the soul thus becomes the center of Ficino's philosophy, because immortality is needed to justify his interpretation of human existence as a continuing effort of contemplation. Without immortality, that effort would be vain, and human existence would be without any attainable end. On the other hand, a philosophy which thus centers around the theory of immortality is primarily concered with man and his purpose, both in the present and in the future life. This concern for man and the immortality of his soul explains certain statements of Ficino which have shocked some modern theologians. For he says that "man worships the eternal God for the sake of the future life," and once he exclaims: "How does it help you, O theologian, to attribute eternity to God, if you do not attribute it to yourself in order that you may enjoy divine eternity through your own eternity?" Ficino also links the doctrine of immortality with the dignity of man when he argues that man, the most perfect of all animals, would be more miserable than the beasts if, through the lack of immortality, he alone were deprived of attaining the natural end of his existence.

The central place in the universe, and the immortality of the soul are privileges in which potentially every human being has a share, yet their actual significance depends on the individual and solitary effort of each person, and on his share in the contemplative life. However, in his theory of love and friendship, Ficino also gives a philosophical significance to the relationship between several persons. He does not condemn or disregard sexual love, to be sure, yet in his famous theory of Platonic love and friendship he is merely concerned with that spiritual relationship which is established between two or more persons through the share which each of them individually has in the contemplative life. In a true friendship, he claims, there are always at least three partners, two human beings, and God who founds their friendship. In this way, Ficino established a direct link between the highest form of human relationship and the most intimate and personal experience of contemplative life. Hence he could proclaim that friendship understood in this sense was the spiritual tie that linked the members of his Platonic Academy with each other and with himself, their common master. This theory of Platonie love and friendship had a tremendous appeal to Ficino's contemporaries and to the successive generations of the sixteenth century who wrote about it again and again in prose and in verse. The term "Platonic love" has since acquired a somewhat curious connotation, and it certainly would be difficult to defend all the vagaries contained in the love treatises of the later Renaissance. However, it is important to realize that the doctrine in its origin had a serious philosophical meaning, and that it was taken up so eagerly because it provided educated persons with a more or less superficial spiritual interpretation for their personal feelings and passions. The rather complex background of the theory which had its roots in ancient theories of love and friendship, in Christian traditions of charity and spiritual fellowship, and in medieval conceptions of courtly love, could only increase its popularity in a period in which all those currents were still very much alive.

For the Florentine Platonists, the concept of man and his dignity was not merely limited to the solitary experiences and to the personal relationships of individuals, but it also led to the conscious awareness of a solidarity of all men which imposed definite moral and intellectual obligations upon each individual. This attitude is implied in Ficino's views about religion and its various kinds. He emphasizes that Christianity is the most perfect religion, to be sure, but he also asserts that religion as such is natural to all men and distinguishes them from the animals. The variety of religions contributes to the beauty of the universe, and each religion, at least in an indirect and unconscious manner, is related to the one, true God. Pico goes even further and emphasizes that all religious and philosophical traditions have a share in a common, universal truth. Pagan, Jewish, and Christian theologians, and also all philosophers who supposedly contradict each other, Plato and Aristotle, Avicenna and Averroes, Thomas and Scotus, and many others have had a good many insights into truth. When Pico included propositions from all these authors among his nine hundred theses, it was his underlying intention to illustrate this universality of truth which justified his endeavor to incorporate and defend doctrines from so many different sources. This syncretism of Pico really provided the foundation for a broad conception of religious and philosophical tolerance.

In a different manner, the solidarity of mankind is expressed in Ficino's conception of *humanitas*. The Latin term is ambiguous since it stands both for the human race, and for humane feeling as a personal virtue. This ambiguity reflects the ancient Roman Stoic idea of *humanitas* that combined with the standards of cultural refinement a high respect for other persons as fellow human beings. This concept was taken up and further elaborated by Ficino. Starting from the general notion that love and attraction constitute a force of unification in all parts of the universe, he applies it in particular to mankind as a natural species. Man proves himself a member of the human race by loving other men as his equals by being humane. When he is inhumane and cruel, he removes himself from the community of mankind and forfeits his human dignity. "Why are boys crueler than old men?" Ficino asks in a letter to Tommaso Minerbetti. "Insane men crueler than intelligent men? Dull men crueler than the ingenious? Because they are, as it were, less men than the others. Therefore the cruel men are called inhumane and brutal. In general those who are far removed from the perfect nature of man by fault of age, a vice of the soul, a sickness of the body, or by an inimical position of the stars, hate and neglect the human species as something foreign and alien. Nero was, so to speak, not a man, but a monster, being akin to man only by his skin. Had he really been a man, he would have loved other men as members of the same body. For as individual men are under one Idea and in one species, they are like one man. Therefore, I believe, the sages called by the name of man himself only that one among all the virtues that loves and helps all men as brothers deriving in a long series from one father, in other words, humanity."

Even Ficino's theory of immortality is influenced by this sense of human solidarity. Ficino admits that the immediate vision of God can be attained in earthly life by a few individuals, but this is not considered as a sufficient fulfillment of the natural desire inherent in all men. The postulate of a future life must be maintained in order that this desire be fulfilled, if not for all men, at least for all those who tried to direct their efforts toward God. Ficino does not teach with Origen that there will be a final salvation of all souls, but he leaves us with the impression that a reasonable proportion of mankind will attain eternal happiness, the true goal of earthly existence and of human life.

The third intellectual current of the early Renaissance, Aristotelianism, had its roots in the teaching traditions of the later Middle Ages. At the Italian universities, the study of Aristotelian philosophy obtained a permanent place about the end of the thirteenth century. From its very beginning, this study was linked with medicine, not with theology. Consequently, it centered around natural philosophy, and to a lesser extent around logic. The so-called theory of double truth which characterizes the tendency of this school was meant to recognize the authority of the Church in the domain of dogmatic theology, and at the same time to preserve the independence of philosophical thought within the limits of natural reason. These Aristotelian philosophers disagreed among each other on many issues and were divided into several opposing schools, yet they had common problems common source materials, and a common method. In contrast to the humanists and to the Platonists, the Aristotelians represent the solid, professional tradition of philosophy. They dominated the teaching of philosophy down to the end of the Renaissance, and their numerous commentaries and treatises reflect the methods and interests of that teaching. Their share in the intellectual life of the Renaissance was much larger than most scholars seem to realize, and they were by no means as foreign to the new problems of their own times as often asserted. Renaissance Aristotelianism developed without a break from the traditions of medieval Aristotelianism, to be sure, but it also assimilated many significant elements from the humanism and Platonism of its own time.

It is easy to illustrate this with the example of the most famous Aristotelian philosopher of the Italian Renaissance, Pietro Pomponazzi.[6] He had received his training at Padua, and spent his later and most productive years as a professor of philosophy at Bologna. Pomponazzi was thoroughly familiar with the ideas and writings of his medieval predecessors and discussed in part the same problems, with the same method of reasoning, and on the basis of the same texts of Aristotle. Yet he was indebted to the humanists for his knowledge of the Greek commentators of Aristotle, and of non-Aristotelian ancient thought, especially of Stoicism. He also utilized the writings of the Platonists and discussed or appropriated some of their ideas. This affinity of Pomponazzi with the humanists and Platonists of his time is especially apparent in his conception of man.

Pomponazzi's concern for man is already expressed in the fact that, like Ficino, he dedicated one of his most important philosophical works to the problem of immortality. As a result of its highly provocative position, this treatise became the starting point of a lively controversy among Aristotelian philosophers and theologians which continued for many decades. In approaching the problem of immortality, Pomponazzi emphasizes with the Platonists that man occupies a middle place in the universe. "I held that the beginning of our consideration should be this: that man is not of simple but of multiple, not of fixed, but of an ambiguous nature, and is placed in the middle between mortal and

---

[6] [On Pomponazzi and Renaissance Aristotelianism see, in addition to Kristeller's studies, A. H. Douglas, *The Philosophy and Psychology of Pietro Pomponazzi* (Cambridge: Cambridge University Press, 1910).]

immortal things. . . . Hence the ancients rightly placed him between eternal and temporal things, since he is neither purely eternal nor purely temporal, because he participates in both natures. And existing thus in the middle, he has the power to assume either nature."

Yet in spite of this starting point, Pomponazzi proceeds to an analysis that in many respects is the exact opposite of Ficino's. The human intellect is not material in its substance, to be sure, but its knowledge is entirely limited to corporeal objects. This is the manner in which it occupies a middle place between the pure intelligences of angels and the souls of animals. There is no evidence whatsoever that man in this life can attain a pure knowledge of intelligible objects. Consequently, there is no rational proof for the immortality of the soul, although immortality must be accepted as an article of faith.

Pomponazzi thus demolishes the ideal of contemplation which finds its necessary fulfillment in a future life. He substitutes for it the ideal of a moral virtue which can be attained during the present life. Thus the dignity of man is not only maintained, but man's present, earthly life is credited with a significance that does not depend on any hopes or fears for the future. Pomponazzi states this view in simple sentences that remind us of Plato and the ancient Stoics as well as of Spinoza and Kant.

There are two kinds of reward and punishment: one is essential and inseparable, the other accidental and separable. The essential reward of virtue is virtue itself which makes man happy. For human nature cannot attain anything higher than virtue. It alone makes man secure and removed from all trouble. . . . The opposite applies to vice. The punishment of the vicious person is vice itself which is more miserable and unhappy than anything else. . . . Accidental reward is more imperfect than essential reward, for gold is more imperfect than virtue; and accidental punishment is less heavy than essential punishment. For a penalty is an accidental punishment, whereas guilt is an essential punishment. Yet the punishment of guilt is much worse than that of a penalty. Therefore, it does not matter if sometimes the accidental is omitted provided that the essential remains. Moreover, when a good received an accidental reward its essential good seems to decrease and does not remain in its perfection. For example, if someone does a good deed without a hope of reward, and another with a hope of reward, the action of the latter is not considered as good as that of the former. Hence he who receives no accidental reward is more essentially rewarded than he who does. In the same way, he who acts wickedly and receives accidental punishment seems to be less punished than he who receives no accidental punishment. For the punishment of guilt is greater and worse than that of a penalty. And when a penalty is added to guilt, the latter decreases. Hence he who receives no accidental punishment is more essentially punished than he who does.

The emphasis on moral virtue as the self-contained end of human life sets, in the first place, a standard of individual conduct. Yet Pomponazzi, like Ficino, arrives quite consistently at the notion that there is a solidarity of mankind, and that each individual, through his right actions, makes his contribution to the universal good. "We must assume and firmly keep in mind that the entire human race may be compared to one individual man." All individuals contribute to the good of mankind, just as all members of our body contribute to the welfare of the entire body. "The whole human race is like one body composed of various members which have different functions, but which are suited for the common usefulness of mankind."

Hence the end of man must be determined in such a way that it can be attained by all men or at least by many individuals. This consideration prompted Ficino to postulate a future life in which many individuals will reach the vision of God which in the present life is experienced only by a few rare persons. The same consideration leads Pomponazzi to assert that the primary aim of human life must be found in moral action, and not in contemplation. This statement is the more interesting since it is at variance with the teaching of Aristotle. All men, Pomponazzi argues, share to some extent in three intellectual faculties, that is, in the speculative, the moral, and the technical intellect. Yet the part which men have in these intellectual faculties is different for each of them. The speculative intellect is not characteristic of man as man, but belongs properly to the gods, as Aristotle says. Although all men have something of it, only very few possess it, or can possess it, fully and perfectly. On the other hand, the technical intellect is not characteristic of man since it is also shared by many animals.

Yet the practical intellect truly belongs to man. For every normal human being can attain it perfectly, and according to it a person is called good or bad in an absolute sense, whereas according to the speculative or technical intellect, a person is called good or bad only in some respect and with qualifications. For a man is called a good man or a bad man with regard to his virtues and vices. Yet a good metaphysician is not called a good man, but a good metaphysician, and a good architect is not called good in an absolute sense, but a good architect. Therefore, a man is not angry when he is not called a metaphysician, a philosopher, or a carpenter. Yet he is most angry when he is said to be a thief, intemperate, unjust, foolish, or something wicked of that sort, as if to be good or bad were human and in our power, whereas to be a philosopher or an architect is not in our power nor necessary for a man. Hence all human beings can and must be virtuous, but not all must be philosophers, mathematicians, architects, and the like. . . . Hence with regard to the practical intellect which is peculiar to man each man must be perfect. For in order that the entire human race be properly preserved each person must be morally virtuous and as much as possible free of vice. . . .

It has been my intention to show that the three major intellectual currents of the early Renaissance were all concerned with the purpose of human life and with the place of man in the universe, and that this concern found its expression not only in definite standards for individual conduct, but also a strong sense for human relationships and for the solidarity of mankind. The humanistic movement which in its origin was not philosophical provided the general and still vague ideas and aspirations as well as the ancient source materials. The Platonists and Aristotelians who were professional philosophers with speculative interests and training, took up those vague ideas, developed them into definite philosophical doctrines, and assigned them an important place in their elaborate metaphysical systems.

After the first quarter of the sixteenth century, the intellectual currents of the earlier Renaissance continued to exist, but they were increasingly overshadowed, first by the theological controversies growing out of the Reformation, and later by the developments that led to the rise of modern science and of modern philosophy. Yet the early Renaissance left a heritage that remained effective at least down to the end of the eighteenth century: Renaissance humanism remained alive in the educational and literary traditions of Western Europe and in the study of history and philology; Renaissance Platonism handed down the influence of Plato and Plotinus to all those thinkers who attempted to defend some idealistic form of philosophy; and Renaissance Aristotelianism, although partly superseded by experimental physics and science, gave inspiration to many later currents of free-thought. In the last century in which so much of our present thought has its origin those older ideas and traditions were largely forgotten, except by a few scholarly specialists. Modern positivism, encouraged by scientific progress and material success, seemed to have made all other ideas more or less obsolete. Yet the startling events of our own time have shaken our confidence in the sufficiency, if not in the truth, of positivism. We wonder whether its principles are broad enough to explain our experience and to guide our endeavors. We have become more modest about our own achievements, and hence more willing to learn from the past. In the long line of philosophers and writers who constitute the history and tradition of Western thought, a distinctive place belongs to the humanists, Platonists, and Aristotelians of the early Italian Renaissance. Many of their ideas are merely a matter of historical curiosity, but some of them contain a nucleus of permanent truth and might thus become a message and an inspiration to present-day Italy, and to the rest of mankind.

PROTESTANTISM AND PROGRESS *

Ernst Troeltsch †

The Meaning of "The Modern World"

Of the historical conceptions with which our inquiry has to deal, one which is apparently among the simplest, but in reality is often rather loosely used, is that of the "modern world"—or, if we wish to avoid the pretentious term "world," which extends rather unduly the sphere of our own existence, the conception of modern civilisation as developed in Europe and America. It will be advisable at the outset to seek a more exact definition of this term, for when this is found it will suggest to us the questions which we shall have to put to Protestanism as one of the ancestors of modern civilisation. This civilisation, of course, includes within itself the most various tendencies, but it bears nevertheless a certain general stamp, of which we are instinctively conscious. The designation "modern" is in this connection to be understood only *a potiori*, since it continues to include a large proportion of the older factors; but it is precisely in the struggle with those older

* Reprinted from *Protestantism and Progress. A Historical Study of the Relation of Protestantism to the Modern World* by Ernst Troeltsch, pp. 9–11, 17–22, 58–62, 64–65, 69–70, 74–75, 85–87, 89–90, 106, 108–117, 128, 131–139, 149–150, 155–157, 159–162 (New York: G. P. Putnam's Sons, 1912).

† Ernst Troeltsch (1865–1923) was Professor of Theology at the University of Heidelberg, and Under-Secretary of State in the Ministry of Public Worship in the Weimar Republic. His publications include the monumental *Social Teaching of the Christian Churches*.

factors that it becomes conscious of its individuality. This individuality, however, is very difficult to define, partly because of the manifoldness and heterogeneity of the factors and conditions which characterise it, partly because of the want of a strict *differentia*, such as might be afforded when the contrast with a different subsequent civilisation had made it possible to recognise the forces which, at the close quarters of present experience, cannot all be brought into the field of vision, or, at any rate, do not fall into proper perspective. We are therefore, for the most part, reduced to defining it by contrast with preceding periods, especially with the immediately preceding period, of civilisation. Thus the characteristics by which we have to define it are essentially negative. Modern civilisation, indeed, first became conscious of its newness by its antithetic relation to that which preceded it; while its attempts to produce something new took the most varied forms. And even at the present day a general characterisation of it can only be given by negative determinations of this kind.

Modern civilisation, if we look to its immediate context, took its rise from the great period of Church civilisation,[1] based on the belief in an absolute and immediate Divine revelation and the embodiment of this revelation in the Church as the organ of redemption and moral discipline. . . .

In contrast with this the essential character of modern civilization becomes apparent. It is everywhere engaged in opposing Church civilisation and in substituting for it ideals of civilisation independently arrived at, the authority of which depends on their inherent and immediate capacity to produce conviction. This independence, whatever its basis, as opposed to Church authority, to purely external divinely-given standards, dominates everything. Even where new authorities are in principle established, or in practice followed, the respect accorded to them arises from purely independent and rational conviction; and even where the older religious convictions hold their ground, their truth and their binding force are, at least among Protestants, primarily based on inner personal conviction, not on submission to authority as such. . . .

When an endeavour was made to find objective standards and fixed points to oppose to mere subjective caprice, scientific thought presented itself as the only resource. In virtue of its foundation in natural science,

[1] [For further elaboration of what Troeltsch meant by "the great period of Church-civilisation," see his larger study *The Social Teaching of the Christian Churches* (London: Allen & Unwin, 1931). The first volume deals with the Middle Ages, the second with the Reformation.]

which was in principle new in relation to antiquity and its products, it offered new potentialities for the establishment of a clearly and methodically defined point of view, as well as for the technical mastery of nature. In the place of revelation, reigned scientific thought, and in place of ecclesiastical authority, the literature inspired by the new methods. Hence the rationalistic, scientific character of modern civilisation, in which its individualism both freely expressed itself, and at the same time seemed to find its natural boundaries. The successor of theology, at once its contrast and its counterpart, was found in the naturalistic, rationalistic system of the sciences and the regulation of life by the so-called Rationalism.

Of course, Individualism could not be always and everywhere kept within these boundaries. The more the supposedly fixed rational order was made the object of historical thought with reference to its origin, and the more historical thought extended itself in the process beyond scientific thought in the narrower sense, the more completely was the fixed system dissolved into the flux of transience, with ever greater future possibilities opening before it. The independence of thought which came in along with Rationalism finally recognised that everything which was ostensibly rational was historically conditioned, and discovered the wide range of variation in professedly rational conceptions. This rationalistic Individualism passed more and more into a Relativism, the disruptive and divisive effects of which are only too familiar to us to-day, but in which we also recognise a liberation of the most tremendous forces and possibilities.

There are not wanting, of course, socialising reactions against this divisive tendency, both in theory and, more especially, in the practical phenomena of political and economic life. But these reactions rest on a different basis from the Church's "authority" civilisation. . . .

Protestantism and the Modern World

There can, of course, be no question of modern civilisation's having been produced simply and solely by Protestantism.[2] All that comes into

[2] [In addition to works already mentioned, see on early Protestant thought in general and/or its "modern" heritage: Roland H. Bainton, The Reformation of the Sixteenth Century (Boston: The Beacon Press, 1952); Harold J. Grimm, The Reformation Era (New York: The Macmillan Company, 1954); Wilhelm Pauck, The Heritage of the Reformation (Glencoe: The Free Press, 1950); Arthur Cushman McGiffert, Protestant Thought before Kant (New York: Charles Scribner's Sons, 1911).]

question is the latter's share therein. But even this share is nothing simple and homogeneous. It differs in different departments of civilisation, and in them all is something more or less complex and elusive. That is precisely what constitutes the peculiar fascination of the problem, and in order to make this intelligible the opposition between Protestantism and modern civilisation must first be indicated more exactly.

The point of primary importance is that, historically and theologically regarded, Protestantism—especially at the outset in Luther's reform of the Church—was, in the first place, simply a modification of Catholicism, in which the Catholic formulation of the problems was retained, while a different answer was given to them. It was only gradually that out of this new answer developed consequences of radical importance for the history of religion, and only when the breach with the first form of Protestantism occurred did it appear how far these consequences went beyond a mere new answer to old problems. That, however, only comes into question later. Protestantism was at first concerned only with the answer to the old question about *assurance of salvation*, which has as its presuppositions the existence of God, and His personal and ethical being, and in general the whole Biblical and medieval cosmology, and has as its only and pressing problem, how, in the face of the condemnation of all men to Hell in consequence of original sin, and in view of the weakness and nothingness of all human and creaturely strength, deliverence from the Judgment, eternal blessedness, and on earth a peace of heart corresponding thereto, secure in its hopes, can be obtained. This is, through and through, the old question which the teaching and discipline of Catholicism had impressed more and more deeply upon men's hearts. Protestantism, instead of pointing to the hierarchic redemptive organisation of the Church and its priesthood, and to the *opus operatum* of the sacraments, supported by the will, answers the question by pointing to a simple radical and personal decision to believe, which, if it be really made in earnest, can assure itself, once for all, from the supernatural Divine revelation of the Bible, of the forgiveness of sins in Christ, and which, on the basis of this certainty, produces all the ethical consequences of reconciliation with God and spiritual union with God. The decisive act of faith receives deliverance purely as an objective assurance of salvation, through the Bible, thus excluding all human effort and making salvation independent of man and dependent on God alone. And the dependence of salvation solely upon God makes it *ipso facto* absolutely certain, and removes it

from the uncertainties and limitations of human action. But since even in
this decision to believe these seems to be some kind of human action or
contributory condition, this decision is itself referred to an immediate
Divine action. In the interest of assurance of salvation the doctrine of
Predestination becomes the central doctrine of Protestantism—whether
with Luther, Zwingli, or Calvin, equally original and equally
necessary. . . .

If the old interest of the certainty of salvation stands in this way in
the centre, and if assurance is reached through a more inward and
spiritual conception of salvation as well as by a more inward appropria-
tion of it, it follows as a matter of course that the old fundamental
idea of wholly authoritative purely Divine ordinances of salvation is
retained. Along with the miracle of redemption, delivering sinners from
darkness and helplessness, there continues also its correlative and continuation, the miricle of the organ of redemption, the Church. Protestantism desired to reform the Church as a whole, and was only forced
against its will to set up Churches of its own. These became national
Churches simply because Protestantism could only realise its ideal of
the Church with the aid of governmental authority, and therefore had
to be content not to apply it beyond the national frontiers. It never
surrendered the thought of the Church itself as the supernatural organ
of salvation, which brings men redemption and orders their life. . . .

All this, therefore, certainly implies, as it was previously implied in
Catholicism, a Church-directed civilisation; indeed here, where there
was no distinction of higher and lower planes of Christian morals, it
is still more strictly applied. The idea is that of a theocracy or, more
exactly, of a "Bibliocracy." No doubt the form through which the
theocratic government is exercised is now quite different. It is no longer
a hierarchy issuing its commands to the civil authority, but a "Bibliocracy" realised by the harmonious combination of spiritual and secular
authorities. In this root-idea the two Confessions are entirely at one. . . .

In all this the Catholic idea of a supernaturally directed civilisation
is continued. And still another characteristic of this civilisation survives,
viz. asceticism. No doubt it is usual to account it a special merit of
Protestantism that it made an end of asceticism and restored secular
life to an honourable status. But it is only necessary to remember that
Protestantism retained in the strictest fashion the determination of
life by the antithesis of heaven and hell, that by abolishing the halfway
house and postponing interval of purgatory, it made them only more
impressive than before, that its central question regarding the assurance

of salvation is expressly concerned with eternal deliverance from original sin. We have only, further, to note that Protestantism even accentuated the Augustinian dogmas of absolute original sin and the complete natural corruption of all man's powers—and we shall have to admit that the inevitable implications of the ascetic idea have here not disappeared but only changed their form and direction. And that is, indeed, the fact. The change is here, as in the case of the other alterations introduced by Protestantism, a vast one, pregnant with consequences, but for all that, there remains an element which—at least in this form—is foreign to the world of to-day, an element which Protestantism has in common with medieval "other-worldly" religion. . . .

If all these considerations be taken into account, it becomes obvious that Protestantism cannot be supposed to have directly paved the way for the modern world. On the contrary, it appears at first, in spite of all its great new ideas, as a revival and reinforcement of the ideal of authoritatively imposed Church-civilisation, as a complete reversion to medieval thinking, thus sweeping away such beginnings of a free and secular civilisation as had already been toilsomely established. Goethe compared it to the French Revolution: "It turned back the advance of quiet culture." And, in addition, it supplied the incentive to a revival of the Catholic idea, and so, in spite of the contemporary diffusion of the ideas and manners of the Renaissance, Europe had to experience two centuries more of the medieval spirit. It is true that anyone who approaches the subject from the side of political or economic history, will not receive this impression, since in these departments the movements which began in the late Middle Ages continued to develop without a break, and, indeed, to a large extent took Protestantism into their service. But anyone who approaches it from the side of the history of religion, of social ethics or of science, will not be able to escape the impression that it was only the great struggle for freedom at the end of the seventeenth and in the eighteenth century which really brought the Middle Ages to an end.

But this only makes it a more pressing question how, in spite of all that, Protestantism could play a conspicuous part in the production of the modern world. As to the fact of its influence there can be no question. The paradox is explained if we follow the hint which this statement of the problem gives us, and seek its influence at first not in a universal regeneration or reconstruction of life as a whole, but mainly in indirect and unconsciously produced effects, nay, even in accidental side-influences, or again in influences produced against its will, particularly if we take into account, alongside of Protestantism proper, the effects of the humanistic criticism which was bound up with it, the ideal of the Baptist sectaries, and the mystical subjectivism. . . .

.   .   .   .

The circumstance which strikes the eye first and foremost is that Protestantism, by breaking up the absolute autocracy of the Catholic Church, broke the power of Church-civilisation, in spite of its temporary revival, once and for all. Three infallible "Churches," unchurching and anathematising one another, discredited the idea of the Church, for which there is no plural. The sixteenth and seventeenth centuries are no longer the Middle Ages, but neither are they "Modern Times." They are the "Confessional" Age of European history, and it is only as a consequence of the mutual attrition—by no means, it must be said, complete—of these three supernatural bodies that the modern world has arisen, a world which knows, indeed, the supersensible, but not the supernatural in the medieval sense. Thus Protestantism disintegrates the Christian Church-system and its supernatural foundation, wholly against its will, but by its actual and ever more clearly apparent influence. The plurality of the Churches and their embittered struggle did more than anything else to multiply the "Libertinists and Neutralists." . . .

The secular State and the modern idea of the State, and an independent political ethic, are not creations of Protestantism.[3] What is true is that it freed the State from all and every kind of subordination to the hierarchy; it taught men to regard civil callings as direct service of God and not as indirect service through the intermediary of the Church. That signifies the final—both formal and theoretical—independence of the State. But it nevertheless is not yet equivalent to the modern idea of the State. So far from that, Protestantism regarded the State as a religious institution, and saw its end and aim in the protection of the Christian commonwealth and the moral law. . . .

Protestantism intervened in the development of the State in the direction of autonomy, and powerfully furthered it. In particular, it invested the expanding civil officialdom with the character of a God-ordained calling, which plays its part in the execution of the Divine will;

----

[3] [On Protestant political thought see John Neville Figgis, *The Divine Right of Kings* (Cambridge: Cambridge University Press, 1914); and J. W. Allen, *A History of Political Thought in the Sixteenth Century* (London: Methuen & Co., 1928).]

and it thus gave to the new centralised administration a strong ethical reinforcement. Then, too, by directly inciting the State to work for the advancement of civilisation, spiritual and material, in the interests of the Christian commonwealth, it inspired the civil government to set before it the widest civilising aims, and put into its hands the care of education, moral order, oversight of food supply, and spiritual and ethical well-being. This is not quite the modern idea of the State as the organ of civilisation, for all this is done by the State in its joint exercise of spiritual authority and in the discharge of Christian duty. But out of it, by the separation of civilisation from the Church, while the civilising functions are retained by the State, there arises the modern idea of the State as the organ of civilisation. . . .

In all this, Protestantism is only strengthening impulses which were already present. Of a more marked character was its influence on the State in regard to form and constitution. That applies, however, in the main, only to Calvinism. In this point the two Confessions differ fundamentally. Everything depends here upon the form given, in the one case and the other, to the Law of Nature as adopted in the churches, just as that had been the decisive factor previously in the Catholic system. Lutheranism, in its conception of the Law of Nature, is thoroughly conservative; and in its complete confidence in God's providence it regards the powers called into being in the natural course of things as *ipso facto* instituted by God and commissioned to be the protectors of the *justitia civilis*. The Old Testament, moreover, supported this theory, by representing Saul and David as appointed by God. God is the *causa remota* of the constituted authorities, and consequently men owe them, as powers whose authority is directly or indirectly derived from God, an unconditional obedience. In virtue of this conception Lutheranism facilitated the transition from the State-authority of the privileged orders to a Territorial abolutism; and by putting Church authority also into its hands, immensely increased the resources of this absolutism. . . .

Quite different was the development of the political spirit of Calvinism. Generally speaking, its State-adaptation of the Law of Nature is at bottom also conservative, though where it has open to it the possibility of the free choice and constitution of new authorities, it prefers a modified aristocracy, as is not surprising in view of its original connexion with the Genevan republic, and the prominence which it gives to the aristocratic idea of predestination. But in its great struggles with the Catholic governments which proscribed the pure word of God, that is to say, the Huguenot, Netherlandish, Scottish, and English struggles, Calvinism gave a much more radical development to its Law of Nature. It successfully established the principle of the right of resistance, which must be exercised on behalf of the word of God in the face of ungodly authorities, the exercise of which becomes the duty of the *magistrats inférieurs* as the next in order as holders of the Divine commission, while, failing these, it must be put in practice even by the individual; indeed, in virtue of a special individual call thereto, the assassination of a tyrant is permissible, as in the case of Jael and Sisera.

This more radical conception gives to the Calvinistic Law of Nature a tendency towards progress, an impulse to reorganise governmental conditions when these were of an "ungodly" character. Moreover, in these attempts at reorganisation themselves, there appears a specifically Reformed idea of the State. For in all such reorganisations the germ-cell was the Reformed presbyterial and synodical Church-order, with its representative system. Thus, in the natural course of things, this system tended towards the theory that the State ought to be reorganised—the State itself must be built up on representative lines and ruled by a *collegium* consisting of those put forward as the "best" by the choice of the electors. Under the influence of these ideas, as has been pointed out especially by Gierke, the Calvinistic conception of the Law of Nature took up into itself the idea of the State-contract. On these lines the *Lex Naturae* leads by the logic of events to a constitution and choice of authorities based on contract. . . .

The democratising of the modern world ought not to be solely and directly referred to Calvinism. The Rationalism which, wholly dissociated from religious considerations, appealed to the pure Law of Nature, has in this connexion a much stronger significance; but all the same, Calvinism took a prominent part in preparing the way for the upgrowth of the democratic spirit. . . .

. . . .

When we turn to the development of economic life and thought, we again become aware of a powerful influence.[4] . . .

A much greater importance in this respect must be attributed to Calvinism. Here, as in politics, it is the power which stands nearer to

[4] [On Protestant economic thought, and especially the relationship between Protestantism and capitalism, the classic works are Max Weber, *The Protestant Ethic and the Spirit of Capitalism* (London: Allen & Unwin, 1930); and R.H. Tawney, *Religion and the Rise of Capitalism* (London: John Murray, 1926).]

the modern world. It has, indeed, always been emphasised that Calvin and his successors rejected the Canon-law prohibition of interest, and did away with the burdensome restrictions on investment; that Geneva, with the support of the *Vénérable Compagnie,* established a bank and introduced industries; that the Calvinistic countries and settlements everywhere show the expansion of industrialism and capitalism. This, however, is not a complete account of the matter. The real significance of Calvinism for the modern economic development which culminates in the all-embracing capitalistic system of the present day lies much deeper. It has lately been pointed out by Max Weber, who, in the course of his investigation of the great main problem of present-day economic history, the problem of the character and origin of capitalism, raised the question regarding the spiritual, ethical, and philosophical presuppositions of this system. Without a definite mental and spiritual background, a system of this kind cannot become dominant, or as Sombart, in dealing with a similar problem, has expressed it: In the minds of the mass of its supporters, or at least in those of its founders, apart from the external occasions, inducements, and incentives, there must be a basis of definite economic attitude. From the capitalistic system we have to distinguish the "capitalistic spirit," apart from which the former would never have come to exercise such power over men's minds. For this spirit displays an untiring activity, a boundlessness of grasp, quite contrary to the natural impulse to enjoyment and ease, and contentment with the mere necessaries of existence; it makes work and gain an end in themselves, and makes men the slaves of work for work's sake; it brings the whole of life and action within the sphere of an absolutely rationalised and systematic calculation, combines all means to its end, uses every minute to the full, employs every kind of force, and in alliance with scientific technology and the calculus which unites all these things together, gives to life a clear calculability and abstract exactness. This spirit, Weber said to himself, cannot have simply arisen of itself as a necessary concomitant of industrial inventions, discoveries, and commercial gains. For it did not arise with the banking business of the late Middle Ages, with the capitalism of the Renaissance, or the Spanish colonisation—here it had to struggle with an opposing spirit, the conscience as educated by Catholicism, and was forced to strike a compromise. Following this line of thought, Weber was led, by way of conjecture from the fact that capitalism flourishes best on Calvinistic soil, to draw the conclusion that the ethico-religious spirit of Calvinism had a special significance for the arising of this capitalistic spirit. By means of a detailed investigation he showed that it was the Calvinistic asceticism which produced on a large scale, not so much capitalism as the capitalistic spirit on which it was based, and thus created the psychological conditions in which the vast expansion of a system at bottom so contrary to nature as capitalism, could come into being and establish itself firmly—which does not, of course, hinder the fact that capitalism extends its influence over men to whom Calvinism means nothing. . . . When all is said and done, Calvinism remains the real nursing-father of the civic, industrial capitalism of the middle classes. Self-devotion to work and gain, which constitutes the involuntary and unconscious asceticism of the modern man, is the child of a conscious "intramundane" asceticism of work and calling inspired by religious motives. The "spirit of the calling," which does not reach out beyond the world but works in the world without "creature-worship," that is, without love of the world, becomes the parent of a tireless systematically disciplined laboriousness, in which work is sought for work's sake, for the sake of the mortification of the flesh, in which the produce of the work serves, not to be consumed in enjoyment, but to the constant reproduction of the capital employed. Since the aggressively active ethic inspired by the doctrine of predestination urges the elect to the full development of his God-given powers, and offers him this as a sign by which he may assure himself of his election, work becomes rational and systematic. In breaking down the motive of ease and enjoyment, asceticism lays the foundations of the tyranny of work over men. And from the fact that the produce of this work is in no way an end in itself, but advances the general well-being, and that all return which goes beyond an adequate provision for the needs of life is felt to be merely a stimulus to the further employment and increase of it, there results the principle of the illimitability and infinitude of work. On the basis of this economic attitude there arose the early capitalism of the Huguenots, of Holland, England, and America. . . .

How far, in detail, the particular developments, as well as the general fact of the capitalistic system, have grown out of the capitalistic spirit of Calvinism, and what other forces have had a share in producing and strengthening it, need not here be made the subject of further inquiry. It is clear enough without this that the contribution of Protestantism to modern economic development, which is, in point of fact, one of the most characteristic features of our modern world, is to be ascribed, not to Protestantism as a whole, but primarily to Calvinism, Pietism,

and the Sectaries, and that even with them this contribution is only
an indirect and consequently an involuntary one. Above all, the imposing
but also terrible expansion of modern capitalism, with its calculating
coldness and soullessness, its unscrupulous greed and pitilessness, its
turning to gain for gain's sake, to fierce and ruthless competition, its
agonising lust of Victory, its blatant satisfaction in the tyrannical power
of the merchant class, has entirely loosed it from its former ethical
foundation; and it has become a power directly opposed to genuine
Calvinism and Protestantism. . . .

.   .   .   .

The influence of Protestantism on the social structure and the
formation of classes is therefore, so far as it exists at all, mainly indirect
and unconscious. That is not to be wondered at in a movement which
is in essence religious, and it is true of Christianity in general. But it
is a different matter when we turn to the theoretic ethical and metaphysical conception of society, and of the relation between the community and the individual, organisation and freedom. This is the proper
sphere of the social significance of a religious movement, and here
there are in fact important influences of Protestantism to be traced. It
has indeed been described, in terms, sometimes of censure, sometimes
of admiration, as the parent of the Individualism which is characteristic
of the modern world. But as a matter of fact, in this case also, things
are very complicated. It is of course beyond question that its strong
religious Individualism, which, however, was only the continuation of
an aspect of mysticism and late-medieval lay religion, had a quite
extraordinary significance for the arising of modern Individualism. And
the demolition of the authority of the Roman Church, which had
embraced the whole world in its organisation, combined with its own
difficulties in the organisation of a Church authority, destroyed the
prototypal form of the conception of life as dominated by authority.
Nevertheless, in its view of the relation of the individual to the community, which is here fundamental, Protestantism is very far from
being individualistic and non-authoritative. On the contrary, in all
its main branches, it is surprisingly conservative. It nowhere recognises
—except in the radical Anabaptist groups—the idea of equality, and
nowhere preaches the free shaping of society by individuals at their
discretion. . . .

This brings us to the question of the relation of Protestantism to

science.[5] In this department, almost more than in any other, it is
customary to regard it as the pioneer of the modern world. But everything depends here upon understanding rightly wherein this pioneering
consisted. For it cannot be said that Protestantism opened up the way
for the modern idea of the freedom of science, of thought, and of the
press; nor, again, that while retaining science under its control and
censorship, it at least inspired it with new self-consistent impulses and
guided it to new and original discoveries. The most important point is
rather that it destroyed previously existing Church-controlled science,
and secularised, at least from a legal point of view, educational institutions, transferring the censorship of them to government boards, on
which theologians were merely represented along with others. In this
way it became possible to the State to foster science from the point of
view of its own interests, and to proceed on independent lines, when
once its estimate and conception of science ceased to coincide with the
Church's, as it had done in the Confessional period. Further, Protestantism encouraged a certain spirit of historical criticism, which subjected the Catholic ecclesiastical tradition and the current conception
of Church history to a severe and suspicious examination. By this it
both strengthened the spirit of individual criticism generally, and deprived legend and dogma of a large part of their content of fact, and
thus learned to apply to them naturalistic psychological methods.
Finally, in its need of tools for this criticism, and of scientific sources of
strength for its new anti-Scholastic Biblical theology, it took over humanistic studies, and therewith at least the germs of philological
criticism and unbiassed interpretation. . . . In regard to science, in
fact, Protestantism is not distinguished in principle from contemporary
Catholicism, which, indeed, having the advantage of a stronger Renaissance tradition, in some respects did finer and more influential work in
this department. The great scientific discoveries of the age, modern
mathematics and physics, proceed from the Renaissance, and a Platonic
influence from the same source brought Kepler into conflict with the
Church authorities. The foundations of modern anti-Aristotelian philosophy were laid by the Catholic Descartes. The recasting of political and
social science is connected with the names of Machiavelli, Bodin, and
Hobbes, all thinkers who stood aloof from the Confessions.

Now, if Protestantism in its spheres of influence and in its Schools,

[5] [For recent literature on this still debatable subject see Mark Curtis, *Oxford
and Cambridge in Transition 1558–1642* (Oxford: The Clarendon Press, 1959),
Chap. IX, and p. 287.]

especially in the (Confessionally mixed) Netherlands and in England, wearied out with religious struggles, gradually acclimatised this new scientific knowledge, and finally, from the time of Locke and Leibnitz, learned to combine and amalgamate it with its most sacred world of ideas, that is certainly a process of the highest significance, which permanently secured to the Protestant peoples a scientific superiority. It also, as one of its results, gave a strong impulse to the critical development of the French spirit. But it is a very far from simple process, which was accomplished amid the most vehement opposition from the strict, older Protestantism, and only became possible through the emergence in Protestanism of new religious elements—in so far as it was not due to an exactly opposite cause, the enfeeblement of the religious spirit and the reaction from the Confessional period. This complicated process, in its present results, causes the identification of the scientific and critical with the Protestant religious spirit to appear to many to be self-evident. In reality it implies, itself, a decisive recasting and transformation of the whole idea of Protestanism, and therefore only comes into question at a later point, when we have to describe the religious development in the stricter sense. The Protestant religious individualism of personal conviction underwent a process of fusion with scientific knowledge and freedom of thought. But that fact also changed Protestantism fundamentally as compared with its first beginnings. The possibility of the change was inherent in Protestantism; but in order that it might come to pass, modern completely self-directing science must first be born. And it was not born out of Protestantism, but only welded into it; and from the first moment of their interconnexion it has involved Protestantism in severe conflicts, which even down to the present are far from being finally settled. . . .

GALILEO'S PHILOSOPHY OF SCIENCE *

Leonardo Olschki †

I

At the age of twenty-five—the same number of years after Galileo's death—Isaac Newton already held in his mind the solution of the most conspicuous of all the problems on which he ever speculated: gravitation and the calculus. These two principal achievements of Newton's genius are interconnected because the quantitative interpretation of motion as a universal phenomenon implied the conception of the infinitesimal as a mathematical notion. For the human mind there is no better way to catch and describe a body in motion than the method of fluxions by which the space covered by such a body can be calculated by its velocity at every instant.

Just so the young scientist was bringing to fruition in an analytical way the system of knowledge and the methods of science already inaugurated by Galileo Galilei *more geometrico* and with experimental tests. As a young instructor at the university of Pisa, and also at the same age of twenty-five, Galileo had already made the decisive steps which led to a new science of motion and consequently to a new philosophy of nature.[1] These revolutionary changes in science and philosophy depended on some simple rules concerning the fall of bodies,

---

* Reprinted from *The Philosophical Review*, July 1943, pp. 349-365. Copyright 1943 by *The Philosophical Review*. Used by permission of *The Philosophical Review* and Mrs. Leonardo Olschki.

† Leonardo Olschki was Instructor and Professor of Romance Languages at the University of Heidelberg from 1909 to 1932. Afterwards he was Lecturer at Johns Hopkins University and Research Associate in the Department of Oriental Languages at the University of California in Berkeley. He is best known in the United States for his book *The Genius of Italy*.

[1] [On the new "philosophy of nature" and the new science in general see Herbert Butterfield, *The Origins of Modern Science* (New York: The Macmillan Company, 1951); A. C. Crombie, *Augustine to Galileo. The History of Science A. D. 400-1650* (London: Falcon Press, 1952); E. A. Burtt, *The Metaphysical Foundations of Modern Physical Science* (Garden City: Doubleday & Company, 1954); Meyrick Carré, *Phases of Thought in England* (Oxford: The Clarendon Press, 1949); and Alexandre Koyré, *From the Closed World to the Infinite Universe* (Baltimore: The Johns Hopkins University Press, 1957).]

velocity, acceleration, concussion, and the basic propositions of Galileo's dynamics, rather than on astronomical doctrines and cosmological speculations.

The influence of Tycho Brahe, Copernicus, Kepler, and Giordano Bruno, is scarcely perceptible out of the fields of scientific and philosophical specialization. The new, and universal, course of thought and research characteristic of modern civilization is represented by conceptions and methods pertinent to a branch of science apparently even more limited. This circumstance is explained by the fact that the technical specialization of these elementary notions is merely an aspect of Galileo's basic and universal conceptions of motion, matter, inertia, vacuum, and relativity. The intuitive background and the speculative consequences of these conceptions mark the turn in the evolution of science and thought which separates the modern from the antique and mediaeval minds.

Galileo's youthful achievements do not consist in definitely formulated statements or in fundamental propositions of a systematic character. The fragments of his first treatise *de motu*, which he brought to a close almost forty years later near the end of his life, show his determination to detach the whole of the phenomena of motion from its more or less latent philosophical and metaphysical background in order to investigate in a limited field of observation and speculation the single as well as the general problems having reference to the subject.

This is the first modern example of an attempt to create and develop a section of natural science as a single discipline of universal value. It was not Galileo's purpose to correct the mistakes and to rectify the conclusions of the doctrines predominating in his epoch. The passionate ardor of the young scientist refused to compromise or to follow the example of his timid and hesitating precursors who always contented themselves with partial solutions in the practical and theoretical fields of physical research.

All these hesitations, contradictions, and perplexities, which brought inextricable confusion into the science of motion or led it to an impasse, depended upon the traditional and general belief of the metaphysical origin and essence of motion as taught by Aristotelian, Platonic, Neoplatonic, and Thomistic philosophy. In this doctrine all the problems connected with phenomena of this kind presuppose an ontological background and religious implications, even when they are tentatively solved with a quantitative method of investigation as promoted by the

Occamists of the school of Paris.[2] The divine origin of "natural" motion is stated and confirmed in all the systems of Christian philosophy in evident accord with conceptions and doctrines taught in antiquity.

There is perhaps no other section of philosophy in which an agreement so consistent and lasting is to be found as in the ancient and mediaeval definition of motion. The fundamental propositions of Thomas Aquinas in this respect give a clear idea of the intellectual courage and the degree of emancipation which had to be attained in order to achieve the radical secularization of this section of natural philosophy. According to this doctrine, fundamentally uncontradicted, motion had been impressed by the Divine Spirit on the celestial spheres as a quality inherent in the heavenly substance. The ultimate aim of this spherical motion is the "assimilatio ad Deum in causando" and the generation and regulation of all inferior things on behalf of man. In our rigid earthly sphere, however, motion is only a temporary, accidental, "violent" disturbance of a natural order which assigns ceaseless circular motion to the heavenly bodies and to the earth eternal rest.

These few maxims out of the many which determine the scholastic philosophy of nature already reveal the qualitative, finalistic, and metaphysical conception of motion as a fundamental cosmological phenomenon. There is little place left for the discussion of the earthly aspects of motion within this system. A dialectic and deductive chain of arguments can easily harmonize these basic assumptions with the gradation of spiritual and moral values which determines the structure of an orderly and well arranged universe. It has been possible to work out on that basis a more or less coherent philosophy of motion, but never a science of motion.

This is the reason why the precursors of Galileo—the theoretical ones as well as the empirical—always failed to find a common principle which could embrace in a coherent system of knowledge both the qualitative and the quantitative aspects of the problem. Thus the artisans, architects, engineers, and artillerists of the Renaissance were never able to harmonize their problems and experiences with that philosophy of motion. For the same reason the contemporary astronomers were unable to insert into any framework of classical and Christian cosmology the heliocentric system of Copernicus. Tycho Brahe's negative attitude

---

[2] On Galileo's precursors and their doctrines of motion cf. A. Koyré, *Études Galiléennes* (3 vols., Paris, 1939), I, 7 *et seq.* and *passim,* with critical references to the literature concerning this subject.

toward this doctrine and Kepler's hesitations are explained by this fact. The irreconcilable discrepancy between the physical and the metaphysical conception of motion became the crucial problem of the philosophy of nature.

The year 1590 was the climax of this contradictory evolution and one of the most dramatic episodes in the history of ideas. The intellectual situation at that time is impressively represented by two facts characteristic of the new trends in philosophy and science. In that year Giordano Bruno had already published all his principal works partially devoted to a speculative extension of the Copernican doctrine.[3] In all these works in verse and prose Bruno eludes any definite consideration of the cosmological and physical problems of motion and angrily repudiates every attempt at a quantitative interpretation of natural phenomena. In the same year Galileo had already terminated his preparatory treatise on the theory of motion which reveals a trend of speculation proceeding exactly in the reverse order.

By eliminating one after the other most of the speculative elements of the doctrine of motion, or by treating them in a strictly mathematical way, the young scientist opened to systematic investigation the unlimited physical space in which a privileged form of motion has no sense. In that space every sort of motion is only a function of the "gravity" to which everything in nature is subjected—even fire and air—because gravity is the fundamental cause of motion independent of the shape and the "nature" of the mobile body. In this way celestial mechanics becomes only an aspect of the general rules which explain the fall or swimming of bodies, the inclined plane, and the different forms and variations of motion.

It is on this basis that the heliocentric system was transformed into a problem of mechanics and could be inserted into the framework of a mathematical and experimental science. From now on this fundamental cosmological problem is closely connected with Galileo's speculations on the phenomena of motion wherever they might be measured and observed. In separating these investigations from the doctrines and methods in which the science of motion remained enmeshed up to his time, Galileo surpassed all his precursors in intellectual courage and scientific discernment. He accepted and retained some of the old conceptions, but they appear in his thought totally outside of the scholastic

[3] [Giordano Bruno (1548-1600), renegade Dominican monk and philosopher, enthusiastic Copernican, advocate of the doctrine of the plurality of worlds, largely, however, on Platonistic premises.]

net of philosophical and metaphysical implications. Thereby every step toward the clarification of the phenomena of motion brought the young scientist closer to a physical explanation and justification of the Copernican system.

These were both the scientific and the psychological conditions of Galileo's decision to direct toward the sky the telescope he had constructed especially for that purpose. But in doing so he did not discover merely astronomical facts. He found much more than he had dared to expect. A new universe of immeasurable proportions, and far from human knowledge and imagination, was unfolded before his eyes. The infinite—formerly an attribute of God or the playground of visionary philosophies—stood before his eyes as a physical property of the space which appeared for its part and at the same time as an empirical reality and as a cosmological problem. The solar system turned out to be only a section of a universe of such exorbitant dimensions that all the usual notions of great and small, of above and below, became empty words and revealed themselves to be a source of common errors and misleading nonsense.

Adapting his own mind to such an extensive cosmological vision, he taught his reluctant and amazed contemporaries to conceive of the whole firmament as a tiny, faintly shining body immersed in the immensity of space and to imagine beyond the limits of human sight an innumerable quantity of similar astronomical systems. In the face of the different astronomical phenomena revealed by the telescope, all the hierarchy of nobility, in which a gradation of the cosmological worthiness of the celestial bodies and spheres had been established, vanished as a phantom of senseless imagination and turned out to be a prejudice originated—as Galileo says—by a cowardly human anxiety arising from fear of death.

Moreover, soon after these celestial discoveries Galileo abandoned the age-old conception of a perfect cosmic order and confessed to a friend his conviction that "God ordered the movements of the celestial spheres with proportions not only incommensurable and irrational but also totally imperceptible to our mind." On that occasion he compared man to an architect who would have distributed the stars in harmonious proportions if he had been induced to construct the celestial vault, "whilst it seems to us that God had scattered them without any rule, symmetry and elegance, just as if He had disseminated them with the hand of chance."

Expressions of this kind prove the disruptive effect of his discoveries on the traditional and official conceptions of an orderly universe as taught and supported by school and church. When the advocate of his opinions in the *Dialogue on the Principal Systems of the World* asserts that the center of the universe is merely an imaginary and nowhere existing point, and when he teaches that there cannot be essential differences of substance and behavior in the heavenly bodies, including our planet, then the representative of the traditional doctrines bursts into the angry assertion that "this way of thinking leads to the subversion of all natural philosophy and stirs up confusion and disruption in heaven, on earth, and in the whole universe."

The opinion of this fictitious personage is, of course, nothing else than Galileo's own conviction. At the beginning of his career he had recognized that his conception of motion and space was irreconcilable with the Aristotelian and, implicitly, the Platonic and Scholastic philosophy of nature. In the fulness of his years and experiences he denied any possibility of a compromise between his cosmological vision and the doctrines of those schools and traditions. It has been reserved to some of our contemporaries to label Galileo as a Paduan Aristotelian or as a Platonist, and even to stress the influence of Neoplatonism on his conceptions of nature.[4] In reality his fundamental conceptions of motion and matter, of geometry and relativity, are just so many radical steps which took the new philosophy of science and nature definitely out of the traditional schemes of thinking and obsolete methods of investigation.

Some fossil material collected from the last ramifications of scholasticism will never restore to Aristotle the paternity of modern science. The part taken by authentic Platonism in the formation of Galileo's thought is represented by his attempt to imagine an ideal abstract reality ruled by mathematical conceptions. But his method of systematically objectifying natural phenomena through physical experiments and astronomical observations transformed that speculative image of the world into a functional, concrete, and measurable reality which is far beyond the Platonic influence and no longer a derivative of Platonic doctrines. The abstract sphere of absolute validity of his laws of motion is no longer the Platonic ideal world but the physical vacuum, just as Galileo's conception of geometry as being homogeneous with

---

[4] Cf. the author's article on "The Scientific Personality of Galileo" in *Bulletin of the History of Medicine*, XII (1942, 248–273. [See also J. H. Randall, "The Development of the Scientific Method in the School of Padua," *Journal of the History of Ideas*, April 1940, pp. 177–206.]

the unalterable matter runs counter to the most elementary principles of Plato's ontological and cosmological system.

There is little left, indeed, of these doctrines in Galileo's natural philosophy based on the conviction of an universe physically homogeneous and developed into a science of quantities and relations. The epistemological value of mechanics had never been anticipated, much less proclaimed and taught, by any one of his precursors. It would have been denied and opposed by all the schools of philosophy represented in Galileo's era and no less by the most daring and independent spirits who—like Nicolaus Cusanus, Copernicus, or Giordano Bruno—never abandoned the traditional conception of motion. A dialectical compromise or a syncretistic fusion of doctrines like those so frequently attempted in the Middle Ages and the Renaissance was out of the question after Galileo's determination to make the laws of dynamics the starting point of a new philosophy of nature. He knew of Giordano Bruno's failure in adapting, in a merely speculative way, the Copernican system to the emanative doctrines of neoplatonic inspiration, and in attempting to substitute for peripatetic schemes of logic the threadbare artifices of the Lullian thinking machine. He had been warned by different kinds of dialectical tricks which serve—as he says—to accommodate the facts to a preconceived purpose instead of accommodating the purposes to the facts as established.

Thus Galileo's attitude toward the fundamental problems of natural philosophy does not reveal hesitations or contradictions. He started with a decided purpose to ban all metaphysical interferences and philosophical implications from his investigation of mechanical phenomena. He kept the same attitude after his celestial discoveries. To Thomas Campanella, who could not understand this apparent self-mutilation of philosophy, Galileo simply answered that "it is more estimable to find out the truth, even in an insignificant detail, than to speculate extensively on the highest problems without a positive and definite result." His precise historical position is to be explained, not by associating his thought and work with doctrines and methods of the past, but by comparing the intellectual attitudes towards science and philosophy predominating in his era with those which grow out of his specific problems and of his scientific insight.

II

For the first time in the history of science some mechanical problems of cosmic validity appeared entirely separate from a system of learning and philosophy. None of Galileo's precursors conceived of the mechanical problems they fruitlessly tried to solve as principles of universal validity which could explain natural phenomena in the heavens with the same evidence and cogency as those on earth. It was a new and bold conviction, indeed, that a physical experiment, or a small number of relations, proportions, and definitions expressed in mathematical language, would be able to reveal and to explain the phenomena occurring in the infinite variety of nature and the unlimited extension of the universe. The epistemological and methodical justification of this uncompromising, disruptive, and ambitious "new science" was a new and difficult intellectual problem for a generation accustomed to accept or to discuss the most different aspects of natural philosophy within the closed system of Aristotelian categories of classification or within the more flexible framework of the Platonic and emanatist doctrines.

The simple theoretical acceptance of the quantitative, experimental, relativistic way of thinking and investigating obliterated the basic principles of their fundamental conceptions and conclusions. Hence this new science had no authority, support, or confirmation, other than the logical necessity of its mathematical demonstrations and the concrete evidence of its experimental tests. There was no possibility of connecting this method of natural investigation with the deductive, distinctive, dialectical, and analogical procedure which made the Aristotelian system of knowledge an almost gapless texture of orderly cognitions.

Thus Galileo's physical, astronomical, and cosmological doctrines appeared isolated in their own intellectual sphere and suspended in a sort of intellectual vacuum. The new science taught on the one hand some attested facts and a new method for the solution of natural problems; on the other hand it revealed the immeasurable extent of human ignorance and the customary source of millenary errors. By that process Galileo brought his contemporaries, in so far as they were thinking beings, into an unexpected and entirely new intellectual situation. All the knowledge that seemed to have been an almost definitive possession of the human mind was presented now as the far goal of a long and hard intellectual conquest. Galileo taught and warned his contemporaries not to think of natural philosophy in Aristotelian, Peripatetic, Platonic, or Scholastic terms or in the way followed by the philosophers of the Renaissance. But he could not settle into a merely negative attitude while teaching a science of universal extension. He had to substitute for the old schemes of thinking a method equivalent at least both in demonstrative force and in extensive comprehension. We ought, therefore, to discover what was his opinion about the significance and goal of a science which, though so limited and fragmentary, dared to replace the most complete and comprehensive systems of human knowledge.

Galileo's repeated and emphatical assertion that "the whole of philosophy is understood only by God" does not entitle the historian of his thought to qualify him as an agnostic or a sceptic. In spite of these sincere and devout expressions of humility and caution, he undoubtedly aimed at a final understanding of the structure of the world, a problem he admitted to be the most noble in nature and science. An expression like this reveals that he knew what no productive and introspective scientist or scholar ever forgets; namely, that a single statement, an isolated detail, a specialized research, an individual scientific conclusion, takes on significance only if it participates in a general truth of universal value. Without this conviction, and when detached from this universal background, research is merely an idle trouble and a mental sport, or— as Galileo put it—a source of "sagacious inventions for the delight of ingenious spirits."

Apparently his system of science seemed to be without any philosophical foundation and comprehensive outlook. Descartes reproached him with having sought only "the reasons of some particular phenomena" and of having "built without a foundation." The French philosopher reveals by the terms of his critical judgments that he was less emancipated from the traditional ways of thinking than the Italian scientist. Galileo was convinced that he had founded a new philosophy in which the extension and quantity of the initial knowledge was irrelevant. He aspired to the intensity and the stringent evidence of some basic notions supported and developed by the conclusive proceedings of his new methods of science. These notions ought to have the absolute intuitive and demonstrative certitude of mathematical propositions and the forceful evidence of repeatedly tested experiments. In his own words, he hoped his discoveries and doctrines "might serve to tune some pipes of this great but discordant organ which our philosophy is, on which many organists seem to take great pains to the end of reaching a perfect concord: but they do it in vain, because they leave and keep out of tune three or four of the principal pipes to which it is consequently impossible to tune the rest in perfect harmony."

The principal aim of the new methods of science is to restore the philosophical harmony of the human mind by means of a few well tuned fundamental principles of a cogent and simple evidence. One of these few general ideas on which his whole system of science stands is his assumption "that matter is unalterable, *i.e.*, always the same, and that because of its eternal and necessary character it is possible to produce demonstrations of it no less straight and neat than those of mathematics." The ubiquity of matter determines the universal validity of this basic principle of Galileo's natural philosophy, just as the unalterable character of matter justifies, and even requires, mathematical procedure in the interpretation of natural phenomena. Matter and mathematics are mutually interdependent. One of the conclusions reached in one of the fields is valid and cogent also for the other. This is not so much the starting point for a "mathesis universalis" as it is the theoretical foundation of an experimental science which reduces human thought and physical experience to the necessary cogency of mathematical conclusions.

In this way Galileo inaugurated, together with physical science, the physical method of thinking which is congruent to but not identical with mathematical thinking. The few but sure propositions of his mechanics were the points of departure for a new intellectual conquest of the world. In place of a closed system of natural philosophy as represented by the traditional doctrines he offered an outlook with unlimited intellectual expansion, and for the old static image of the world he substituted a new dynamic vision of a steady scientific development. This vision is supported by the eternal belief that God reveals Himself in the majesty of nature. But Galileo believed that God reveals Himself also in our human mind. The privilege of reading in the great book of nature is granted to man on condition that he spell out the mathematical letters in which it is written. Its proper and infallible language excludes the insidious fallacies of the common human tongues and the figurative interpretation of phenomena. It helps to avoid the misunderstandings derived from false analogies, and makes impossible all the wrong conclusions which depend on alogical inferences and the metaphorical sense of words.

To the apparent and delusive knowledge of the traditional philosophies he opposes the intuitive, inexorable, and transparent veracity of the physical principles and methods which are so evident and universal that within their spheres there can be no difference of opinion among men, nor a breach of understanding between man and God. In fact—he says in memorable terms—if taken *extensively* human knowledge is like nothing in comparison with the infinite divine intelligence; but *as to the intensity* of the propositions acquired by the human mind with the mathematical method of thinking there can be no gradation of their objective and necessary certitude. In this field of knowledge the human mind coincides with the divine wisdom with a mere difference of time because the knowledge gradually attained by the investigating human intellect is always omnipresent in the mind of God.

The philosophical consequences and the epistemological implications of this daring and sublime thought are unequivocal and inescapable. It was far from Galileo's intention to put in question the transcendence of the divine mind; but he was convinced of the divinity of human intelligence. Some of the philosophers of the Renaissance went so far as to believe that there was affinity and congeniality between the divine and the human mind. The relationship between both is an old and perhaps inexhaustible religious and theological problem. But nobody had ever presumed to attest their identity within the sphere of a measuring, counting, and weighing science. This objective, impersonal science, proceeding along the track of mathematical conclusions, is able to some extent to attain the absolute divine certainty which was formerly granted only to a few favored seers in an instant of silent mystical rapture. The penetration of the divine mind and the contemplation of the wonders of nature are now possible to all of God's creatures who can adapt their minds to the methods and conclusions of a correct scientific way of thinking.

Although an autonomous creation of the human intellect, by virtue of its divine aim and support science cannot remain isolated in its own field of self-sufficient knowledge. Philosophy, cosmology, theology, and metaphysics cannot overlook the achievements of a science so absolute in its methods and results that it does not admit within its sphere any contradiction between human and divine knowledge. It was from this theoretical and philosophical conviction that Galileo drew the impulse, the courage, and the tenacity, for challenging both the representatives of the official scientific doctrines in schools and the guardians of religious orthodoxy in the ecclesiastical institutions, to face the new spiritual situation following from the incontestable acquisitions of a new science and his discoveries in the sky. Thus he set out to convince his generation of the priority and supremacy of scientific conclusions over all the contradictory results of the speclative and dialectic schools and methods of philosophy and also in cases where contradictions might be found between the two forms of divine revelation, *i.e.*, between the word of God in the Scriptures and the laws of nature in science.[5] Words, he says, even if inspired by God, are ambiguous because they are subject to the limited power of common human comprehension; on the contrary, the inexorable and immutable laws of nature are unequivocal and exactly the same both for divine and human understanding. He firmly believed that even the smallest truth acquired by the human intellect with the methods of science participates in the universal wisdom of God.

It is from this point of view that Galileo insistently asked for a thorough revision of the doctrines then predominating in schools and in general European culture. Simultaneously he warned the theologians not to stick at the words of the Scriptures when they seem to contradict the results of cogent demonstrations and scientific experiments. The time will come—he said—when it would be heretical to say that the earth stands still and the sun moves, *i.e.*, just the contrary of the opinion that they were defending with all the weight of their authority. He was convinced that God's knowledge is infinite times infinite; but he believed in the unlimited progress of science in revealing the secrets of nature with a godlike certitude. "Science can only advance," says the representative of his doctrines in the *Dialogue on the Principal Systems of the World*. And Galileo himself asked emphatically: "Who wants to put limits to the human mind?"

That the truth ripens with time had been a vague feeling since antiquity: *Veritas Filia Temporis*. But this beautiful device took on a new significance when Galileo substituted for the extensive growth of human knowledge the methods of an intensive and progressive science of nature. He knew that one truth draws the next after it, but at the same time he felt that every truth discovered by natural science is a starting point for new speculations and the key to unexpected mysteries. For Galileo science is as unlimited as its object. But every new conclusion attained with its methods represents a new approach of the human to the divine intellect: *Veritas Filia Aeternitatis*.

[5] This idea is extensively explained in the Letter to the Grand Duchess Cristina (1615). [This important letter is reprinted in English translation in Stillman Drake, *Discoveries and Opinions of Galileo* (Garden City: Doubleday & Company, 1957), pp. 173–216.]

The human mind is a part of the divine mind, just as our solar system is a part of the infinite universe. The limits exist only in our understanding, which increases with every conquest of an intensive and infallible science. Consequently no mediator is needed for our cognition of the divine intelligence as soon as we possess the tools supplied by this progressive science. For Galileo metaphysics does not lie beyond physics because physics is a part of metaphysics. Thus theology and natural science have, though their fields and methods are different, an identical goal. On the basis of its unshakable objective principles and with this metaphysical support his rational and empirical natural science became identical with natural philosophy. By its very definition this philosophy does not concern itself with ontological questions. It does not consider being but that which comes to pass. Its interest is directed toward the circumstances and conditions in which a natural phenomenon occurs; but it excludes as totally superfluous inquiries into the essence of things. This philosophy makes nature an object of divine contemplation and human investigation with a mere difference of time as to the essential and necessary results. In the knowledge of the immutable and inexorable laws of nature the divine and the human mind meet in an intimate union which cannot be attained by other means or in a different field of knowledge.

The first implication of Galileo's philosophy of science is a clear separation of science from religion with the effect of securing their coexistence without conflicts of conscience or contradictions in maxims and doctrines. Science has a preeminence in questions concerning the human knowledge of nature, religion in matters of human salvation. If this respective autonomy is mutually accepted there can never be an heretical conclusion in a natural philosophy which is based on irrefragable principles and whose methods lead to a godlike understanding of the universe. Nor can religion hamper the fated advancement of human knowledge.

The traditional science gave a finite image of the universe with some lacunae to be filled in by assiduous collecting of facts, by schemes of logic, or by commonsense evidence. The new science, on the contrary, starting from a personal intellectual experience, proved to be an endless puzzle with some reliable rules for its solution, but without a pattern for its final completion. Galileo's science is conceived as a perennial philosophy of a progressive and dynamic character, as a slow but steady intellectual conquest of the universe. It was the conviction of an intimate, even if partial, conformity of the human and the divine mind that gave this fragmentary and inexhaustible science its moral value and the certainty of its ultimate perfection.

The metaphysical implications of Galileo's philosophy of science exclude every attempt at a pantheistic interpretation of nature. On the other hand the same fundamental assumption frustrates the long effort of the philosophers of the Italian Renaissance from Ficino to Bruno, who sought the solution of the essential problems of natural philosophy in the framework of Platonic doctrines or in the schemes of neoplatonic emanatism. Likewise Galileo's speculations about motion prove that he did not intend to dissolve the entire philosophy of nature into a sort of universal mathematics and to reduce the structure of the universe to a pure geometrical system. He was far from renewing the conception of God as the divine Geometer which Pascal rejected as a pagan philosophical myth. But inevitably this self-assured, inquisitive, and aggressive science, which pretended to attain a godlike knowledge and a sort of preeminence over all other doctrines, profane as well as divine, would clash with dogmas and philosophies inspired by a divine revelation. A formal juridical procedure invoked by Pope Urban VIII seemed sufficient to wipe out a doctrine which dared to limit and constrain the power and wisdom of God within the narrow district of human understanding.

Its final condemnation did not intend to destroy Galileo's new science of motion but to suppress its necessary implications, both cosmological and philosophical. But this discriminating differentiation of science and philosophy turned out to be a dangerous and even fatal delusion. This authoritative reaction against the intellectual hegemony of a natural philosophy based on physico-mathematical methods of investigation deprived the new science of its philosophical support and of its metaphysical "raison d'être." Pushed back into the boundaries of a technical discipline, this powerful instrument of knowledge became a tool in the hands of the *homo faber* as a source of "sagacious inventions for the delight of ingenious spirits." The technical specialization of science led to the spiritual isolation of the human genius. Seen from this angle the divine aspiration of Galileo is not merely an episode in the history of science and philosophy. Now more than ever it appears to be the condition for the success of human efforts in the secular struggle for scientific enlightenment.

THE TOUCH OF COLD PHILOSOPHY *

Basil Willey †

In order to get a bird's-eye view of any century it is quite useful to imagine it as a stretch of country, or a landscape, which we are looking at from a great height, let us say from an aeroplane. If we view the seventeenth century in this way we shall be stuck immediately by the great contrast between the scenery and even the climate of its earlier and that of its later years. At first we get mountain-ranges, torrents, and all the picturesque interplay of alternating storm and brightness; then, farther on, the land slopes down to a richly cultivated plain, broken for a while by outlying heights and spurs, but finally becoming level country, watered by broad rivers, adorned with parks and mansions, and lit up by steady sunshine. The mountains connect backwards with the central mediaeval Alps, and the plain leads forwards with little break into our own times. To drop the metaphor before it begins to be mis-leading, we may say that the seventeenth century was an age of transi-tion, and although every century can be so described, the seventeenth deserves this label better than most, because it lies between the Middle Ages and the modern world. It witnessed one of the greatest changes which have ever taken place in men's ways of thinking about the world they live in.

I happen to be interested in literature, amongst other things, and when I turn to this century I cannot help noticing that it begins with Shakespeare and Donne, leads on to Milton, and ends with Dryden and Swift: that is to say, it begins with a literature full of passion, paradox, imagination, curiosity, and complexity, and ends with one distinguished rather by clarity, precision, good sense, and definiteness of statement. The end of the century is the beginning of what has been called the Age of Prose and Reason, and we may say that by then the qualities necessary for good prose had got the upper hand over those which

* Reprinted from *The Seventeenth Century: Studies in the History of English Thought and Literature from Bacon to Pope*, by Richard Foster Jones and Others, pp. 369–376, with the permission of the publishers, Stanford University Press. Copyright 1951 by the Board of Trustees of the Leland Stanford Junior University.

† Basil Willey was King Edward VII Professor of English Literature at the University of Cambridge. His publications include *The Seventeenth Century Background* and *Nineteenth Century Studies*.

produce the greatest kinds of poetry. But that is not all: we find the same sort of thing going on elsewhere. Take architecture, for example: the Elizabethan or Jacobean style is quaint and fanciful, sometimes rugged in outline, and richly ornamented with carving and decoration in which Gothic and classical ingredients are often mixed up together. By the end of the century this has given place to the style of Christopher Wren and the so-called Queen Anne architects, which is plain, well proportioned, severe, and purely classical without Gothic trimmings. And here there is an important point to notice: it is true that the seventeenth century begins with a blend of mediaeval and modern elements, and ends with the triumph of the modern; but in those days to be "modern" often meant to be "classical," that is, to imitate the Greeks and Romans. We call the Age of Dryden, Pope, and Addison the "Augustan" age, and the men of that time really felt that they were living in an epoch like that of the Emperor Augustus—an age of enlightenment, learning, and true civilization—and congratulated themselves on having escaped from the errors and superstitions of the dark and monkish Middle Ages. To write and build and think like the ancients meant that you were reasonable beings, cultivated and urbane— that you had abandoned the shadow of the cloister for the cheerful light of the market-place or the coffee-house. If you were a scientist (or "natural philosopher") you had to begin, it is true, by rejecting many ancient theories, particularly those of Aristotle, but you knew all the while that by thinking independently and taking nothing on trust you were following the ancients in spirit though not in letter.

Or let us glance briefly at two other spheres of interest: politics and religion. The century begins with Cavalier and Roundhead and ends with Tory and Whig—that is to say, it begins with a division arousing the deepest passions and prejudices, not to be settled without bloodshed, and ends with the mere opposition of two political parties, differing in principle, of course, but socially at one, and more ready to alternate peaceably with each other. The Hanoverians succeed the Stuarts, and what more need be said? The divine right of kings is little more heard of, and the scene is set for prosaic but peaceful development. Similarly in religion, the period opens with the long and bitter struggle between Puritan and Anglican, continuing through Civil War, and accompanied by fanaticism, persecution, and exile, and by the multiplication of hostile sects; it ends with the Toleration Act, and with the comparatively mild dispute between the Deists and their opponents as to whether Nature was not after all a clearer evidence of God than Scripture, and the conscience a safer guide than the creeds. In short, wherever we turn we find the same tale repeated in varying forms: the ghosts of history are being laid; darkness and tempest are yielding to the light of common day. Major issues have been settled or shelved, and men begin to think more about how to live together in concord and prosperity.

Merely to glance at this historical landscape is enough to make one seek some explanation of these changes. If the developments had conflicted with each other we might have put them down to a number of different causes, but since they all seem to be setting in one direction it is natural to suppose that they were all due to one common underlying cause. There are various ways of accounting for historical changes: some people believe, for instance, that economic causes are at the bottom of everything, and that the way men earn their living, and the way in which wealth is produced and distributed, determine how men think and write and worship. Others believe that ideas, rather than material conditions, are what control history, and that the important question to ask about any period is what men then believed to be true, what their philosophy and religion were like. There is something to be said on both sides, but we are concerned with a simpler question. We know that the greatest intellectual change in modern history was completed during the seventeenth century: was that change of such a kind as to explain all those parallel movements we have mentioned? would it have helped that drift towards prose and reason, towards classicism, enlightenment, and toleration? The great intellectual change was that known as the Scientific Revolution, and I think the answer to these questions is, Yes. It is not my present purpose to describe that Revolution, or to discuss any of the great discoveries which produced it. My intention is only to consider some of the effects it had upon men's thoughts, imaginations, and feelings, and consequently upon their ways of expressing themselves.[1] The discoveries—I am thinking mainly of the Copernican as-

[1] [Professor Willey has pursued this intention farther in his *The Seventeenth Century Background* (London: Chatto and Windus, 1934). Other books dealing with "the effects" of the Scientific Revolution are Paul Hazard, *The European Mind 1680-1715* (New Haven: Yale University Press, 1952); Alfred North Whitehead, *Science and the Modern World* (New York: The Macmillan Company, 1925); Richard F. Jones, *Ancients and Moderns* (St. Louis: Washington University Press, 1936); G. N. Clark, *Science and Social Welfare in the Age of Newton* (Oxford: The Clarendon Press, 1937); Louis Bredvold, *The Intellectual Milieu of John Dryden* (Ann Arbor: University of Michigan Press, 1934); and Richard S. Westfall, *Science and Religion in Seventeenth-Century England* (New Haven: Yale University Press, 1958).]

tronomy and the laws of motion as explored by Galileo and fully formulated by Newton—shocked men into realizing that things were not as they had always seemed, and that the world they were living in was really quite different from what they had been taught to suppose. When the crystal spheres of the old world-picture were shattered, and the earth was shown to be one of many planets rolling through space, it was not everyone who greeted this revelation with enthusiasm as Giordano Bruno did. Many felt lost and confused, because the old picture had not only seemed obviously true to common sense, but was confirmed by Scripture and by Aristotle, and hallowed by the age-long approval of the Church. What Matthew Arnold said about the situation in the nineteenth century applies also to the seventeenth: religion had attached its emotion to certain supposed facts, and now the facts were failing it. This note of loss can be heard in Donne's well-known lines:

> And new philosophy calls all in doubt;
> The element of fire is quite put out;
> The sun is lost, and th'earth, and no man's wit
> Can well direct him where to look for it.

Not only "the element of fire," but the very distinction between heaven and earth had vanished—the distinction, I mean, between the perfect and incorruptible celestial bodies from the moon upwards, and the imperfect and corruptible terrestrial bodies below it. New stars had appeared, which showed that the heavens could change, and the telescope revealed irregularities in the moon's surface—that is, the moon was not a perfect sphere, as a celestial body should be. So Sir Thomas Browne could write:

While we look for incorruption in the heavens, we find they are but like the earth;—durable in their main bodies, alterable in their parts; whereof, besides comets and new stars, perspectives begin to tell tales, and the spots that wander about the sun, with Phaeton's favour, would make clear conviction.

Naturally it took a long time for these new ideas to sink in, and Milton still treats the old and the new astronomies as equally acceptable alternatives. The Copernican scheme, however, was generally accepted by the second half of the century.[2] By that time the laws governing the

---

[2] [See on this point Dorothy Stimson, *The Gradual Acceptance of the Copernican Theory of the Universe* (New York: Trade selling agents, Baker and Taylor Co., 1917).]

motion of bodies on earth had also been discovered, and finally it was revealed by Newton that the law whereby an apple falls to the ground is the very same as that which keeps the planets in their courses. The realization of this vast unifying idea meant a complete re-focussing of men's ideas about God, Nature, and Man, and the relationships between them. The whole cosmic movement, in the heavens and on earth, must now be ascribed, no longer to a divine pressure acting through the *primum mobile,* and to angelic intelligences controlling the spheres, but to a gravitational pull which could be mathematically calculated. The universe turned out to be a Great Machine, made up of material parts which all moved through space and time according to the strictest rules of mechanical causation. That is to say, since every effect in nature had a physical cause, no room or need was left for supernatural agencies, whether divine or diabolical; every phenomenon was explicable in terms of matter and motion, and could be mathematically accounted for or predicted. As Sir James Jeans has said: "Only after much study did the great principle of causation emerge. In time it was found to dominate the whole of inanimate nature . . . The final establishment of this law . . . was the triumph of the seventeenth century, the great century of Galileo and Newton." It is true that mathematical physics had not yet conquered every field: even chemistry was not yet reduced to exactitude, and still less biology and psychology. But Newton said, "Would that the rest of the phenomena of nature could be deduced by a like kind of reasoning from mechanical principles"—and he believed that they could and would.

I referred just now to some of the immediate effects of the "New Philosophy"; let me conclude by hinting at a few of its ultimate effects. First, it produced a distrust of all tradition, a determination to accept nothing as true merely on authority, but only after experiment and verification. You find Bacon rejecting the philosophy of the mediaeval Schoolmen, Browne writing a long exposure of popular errors and superstitions (such as the belief that a toad had a jewel in its head, or that an elephant had no joints in its legs), Descartes resolving to doubt everything—even his own senses—until he can come upon something clear and certain, which he finally finds in the fact of his own existence as a thinking being. Thus the chief intellectual task of the seventeenth century became the winnowing of truth from error, fact from fiction or fable. Gradually a sense of confidence, and even exhilaration, set in; the universe seemed no longer mysterious or frightening; everything in it was explicable and comprehensible. Comets and eclipses were no longer dreaded as portents of disaster; witchcraft was dismissed as an old wives' tale. This new feeling of security is expressed in Pope's epitaph on Newton:

> Nature and Nature's laws lay hid in night;
> God said, *Let Newton be!* and all was light!

How did all this affect men's religious beliefs? The effect was very different from that of Darwinism on nineteenth-century religion. In the seventeenth century it was felt that science had produced a conclusive demonstration of God, by showing the evidence of His wisdom and power in the Creation. True, God came to be thought of rather as an abstract First Cause than as the personal, ever-present God of religion; the Great Machine implied the great mechanic, but after making the machine and setting it in motion God had, as it were, retired from active superintendence, and left it to run by its own laws without interference. But at a time when inherited religious sentiment was still very powerful, the idea that you could look up through Nature to Nature's God seemed to offer an escape from one of the worst legacies of the past—religious controversy and sectarian intolerance. Religion had been endangered by inner conflict; what could one believe, when the Churches were all at daggers drawn? Besides, the secular and rational temper brought in by the new science soon began to undermine the traditional foundations of belief. If nothing had ever happened which could not be explained by natural, physical causes, what of the supernatural and miraculous events recorded in the Bible? This was a disturbing thought, and even in the seventeenth century there were a few who began to doubt the literal truth of some of the Biblical narratives. But it was reserved for the eighteenth century to make an open attack upon the miraculous elements in Christianity, and to compare the Old Testament Jehovah disparagingly with the "Supreme Being" or "First Cause" of philosophy. For the time it was possible to feel that science was pious, because it was simply engaged in studying God's own handiwork, and because whatever it disclosed seemed a further proof of His almighty skill as designer of the universe. Science also gave direct access to God, whereas Church and creed involved you in endless uncertainties and difficulties.

However, some problems and doubts arose to disturb the prevailing optimism. If the universe was a material mechanism, how could Man be fitted into it—Man, who had always been supposed to have a free will and an immortal soul? Could it be that these were illusions after

all? Not many faced up to this, though Hobbes did say that the soul
was only a function of the body, and denied the freedom of the will.
What was more immediately serious, especially for poetry and religion,
was the new tendency to discount all the products of the imagination,
and all spiritual insight, as false or fictitious. Everything that was real
could be described by mathematical physics as matter in motion, and
whatever could not be so described was either unreal or else had not
yet been truly explained. Poets and priests had deceived us long enough
with vain imagining; it was now time for the scientists and philosophers
to take over, and speak to us, as Sprat says the Royal Society required
its members to do, in a "naked, natural" style, bringing all things as
close as possible to the "mathematical plainness." Poets might rave, and
priests might try to mystify us, but sensible men would ignore them,
preferring good sense, and sober, prosaic demonstration. It was said at
the time that philosophy (which then included what we call science)
had cut the throat of poetry.[3] This does not mean that no more good
poetry could then be produced: after all, Dryden and Pope were both
excellent poets. But, when all has been said, they do lack visionary power:
their merits are those of their age—sense, wit, brilliance, incisiveness,
and point. It is worth noticing that when the Romantic Movement
began a hundred years later, several of the leading poets attacked
science for having killed the universe and turned man into a reasoning
machine.[4] But no such thoughts worried the men of the Augustan age;
their prevailing feeling was satisfaction at living in a world that was
rational through and through, a world that had been explained favour-
ably, explained piously, and explained by an Englishman. The modern
belief in progress takes its rise at this time; formerly it had been thought
that perfection lay in antiquity, and that subsequent history was one
long decline. But now that Bacon, Boyle, Newton, and Locke had
arisen, who could deny that the ancients had been far surpassed? Man
could now hope to control his environment as never before, and who
could say what triumphs might not lie ahead? Even if we feel that the

[3] [Thus, Jean-Baptiste Rousseau wrote to a friend in 1715: "I have often
said that the philosophy of Descartes had cut the throat of poetry."]

[4] [Keats and Coleridge are in fact the source for the term "Cold Philosophy"
used in the title of this article. Thus Keats in *Lamia*:

> Do not all charms fly
> At the mere touch of cold philosophy?

Coleridge thought that the poet, by means of the imagination, brought to life
an "inanimate cold world."]

victory of science was then won at the expense of some of man's finer faculties, we can freely admit that it brought with it many good gifts as well—tolerance, reasonableness, release from fear and superstition— and we can pardon, and even envy, that age for its temporary self-satisfaction.

THE INFLUENCE OF EIGHTEENTH CENTURY IDEAS ON THE FRENCH REVOLUTION *

Henri Peyre †

No question is likely to divide students of the past more sharply than that of the action of philosophical ideas and literary works upon political and social events.[1] Our age has been powerfully impressed by the economic interpretation of history proposed by Marxists; but it has also witnessed the important role played by men of letters and men of thought in the Spanish Civil War and in the Resistance movement of World War II. The conscience of many writers is more obsessed today than it has ever been by the temptation—some call it the duty—of "engaged literature." The affinities of many of the leading authors in France and other countries link them with the men of the eighteenth century. Sartre, Camus, Giono, Breton are not unworthy descendants or reincarnations of Voltaire, Diderot, Rousseau. It may thus be useful to attempt a restatement of an old, and ever present, problem, without any presumptuous claim to renovate its data or its solution, but with an honest attempt to observe a few conditions which are obvious but all

* Reprinted from the *Journal of the History of Ideas,* Jan. 1949, pp. 63–87. Copyright 1949 by the *Journal of the History of Ideas.* Used by permission of the *Journal of the History of Ideas* and the author.

† Henri Peyre is Sterling Professor of French and was for many years Chairman of the Department of Romance Languages at Yale University. His publications include *Les Générations Littéraires* and *The Contemporary French Novel.*

[1] [Professor Peyre's article contains a number of references to historians who have studied the impact of ideas on the French Revolution, notably Hippolyte Taine and Daniel Mornet. For further discussion of their views, see Richard Herr, "*Histoire Littéraire:* Daniel Mornet and the French Enlightnment," *The Journal of Modern History,* June 1952, pp. 152–166.]

too seldom met. A summation of such an immense and thorny question should be clear, while respecting the complex nature of reality. It should be provocative, in the sense that it should suggest that much remains to be said on these matters by young scholars determined to launch upon the study of ideas in relation to the Revolution. Above all, it should be impartial if that is humanly possible, concerning questions on which it is difficult not to take sides, and it should attempt to retain in these questions the life with which they are instinct, without on the other hand sacrificing objectivity or solidity.

I

The problem of the effect of the Philosophy of Enlightenment [2] on the French Revolution is one of the most important problems that confront the pure historian as well as the historian of thought and of literature. It is without doubt the most complex of the thousand aspects involved in the study of the Revolution, that is to say the origins of the modern world. Together with investigation of the origins of Christianity and the end of the ancient world, this study concerns one of the two most important upheavals that the philosophically-minded historian can conceive: Taine and Renan, as well as Michelet and Tocqueville, the four most important French historians of the past century, had quite rightly realized its magnitude. This problem is inevitable for every teacher of literature who lectures on Voltaire and Rousseau to his students, for every historian of the years 1789–1799 in France, and likewise for every historian of these same years and of the beginning of the nineteenth century in Germany, England, the United States and Latin America. It presents itself to every voter who reflects even a little about the things in his country's past that he would like to maintain and those that he desires to reform.

[2] [On the Enlightenment see, in addition to the books and authors mentioned by Peyre, the following general works: Preserved Smith, *A History of Modern Culture,* Vol. II (New York: Henry Holt, 1930–1934); Ernst Cassirer, *The Philosophy of the Enlightenment* (Princeton: Princeton University Press, 1951); Paul Hazard, *European Thought in the Eighteenth Century* (New Haven: Yale University Press, 1954); and Lester Crocker, *Age of Crisis. Man and World in Eighteeth Century French Thought* (Baltimore: Johns Hopkins University Press, 1959).

On the interpretation of the Enlightenment Carl Becker's famous book *The Heavenly City of the Eighteenth-Century Philosophers* (New Haven: Yale University Press, 1932) should also be consulted, as well as the critique of Becker's thesis by Peter Gay and others in R. O. Rockwood (ed.), *Carl Becker's Heavenly City Revisited* (Ithaca: Cornell University Press, 1958).]

But because it presents itself so insistently to everyone, this problem has often been met with solutions that are crude or at the very least lacking in necessary overtones; because it closely parallels our present-day preoccupations, it has aroused the partisan spirit; because it concerns not only facts but ideas it has favored excessively dogmatic generalizations on the one hand and on the other, the voluntary blind timidity of chroniclers who have chosen to see in the events of the Revolution nothing but a series of improvisations and haphazard movements.

There is for one thing a long and devious current of ideas which first springing forth as a swift and turgid torrent in the sixteenth century, becoming a more or less tenuous water-course in the great period of the reign of Louis XIV, and finally like a river encircling the most obdurate islets of resistance within its multiple arms, seems to have engulfed the eighteenth century in the years 1750–1765. More and more clearly, those who set forth and develop these ideas take it upon themselves to influence the existing facts, to change man by education, to free him from out-moded superstitions, to increase his political liberty and his well-being. In no way do they dream of a general cataclysm and several of them are not insensitive to the refined amenity of the life that surrounds them or to the exquisite blend of intellectual boldness and voluptuous refinement that characterizes their era.

Suddenly, this pleasant 18th-century security, "Table d'un long festin qu'un échafaud termine," as Hugo's beautiful image calls it, crumbles. The Revolution breaks out, and within a few years, rushes through peaceful reforms, produces a profusion of constitutions, sweeps aside the old regime, devours men, and causes heads to fall. This great movement is certainly confused, turbulent and irrational like everything that men accomplish by collective action. However, lawyers, officers, priests, and journalists play a part in it that is often important. These men had grown up in an intellectual climate that had been established by Montesquieu, Voltaire, Rousseau, Raynal and Mably. May we accurately reach a conclusion of "Post hoc, ergo propter hoc"?

It would not have been so difficult to answer such a question if partisan quarrels had not needlessly clouded the issue. Frenchmen are incapable of viewing their nation's past dispassionately or accepting it as a whole. For a hundred and fifty years they have not ceased to be of different minds on their Revolution which is doubtless a proof that it is still a live question among them, while in other countries the revolution

of 1688 or the revolution of 1776 is calmly invested with the veneration
accorded to a buried past. It is a curious fact that the great majority of
their political writers from Joseph de Maistre, Louis de Bonald, and
Auguste Comte himself, to Le Play, Tocqueville, Taine, at times
Renan, Barrès, Bourget, Maurras and many others, has pronounced
itself hostile to the "great principles of '89" or at least to that which was
drawn from these principles. Three fundamental assertions are the basis
of most of the anti-revolutionary arguments. A) The Revolution was
harmful and anti-French; it could only be attributed to foreign influences that perverted the French genius of moderation, restrained de-
votion, and obedience to the hereditary monarch. It was caused by
foreign influences that contaminated eighteenth century thought:
Locke, the English deists, the Protestants in general, the Swiss Rousseau, etc. . . . B) These corrupting ideas were introduced among the
French people who had been sound and upright until then, by clubs
called "Sociétés de Pensée" and by secret groups of conspiring intellectuals, the Freemasons for example and the "Philosophes" themselves,
who formed an authentic subversive faction. (Augustin Cochin, Les
Sociétés de Pensé, Plon, 1921.) C) The Revolutionary spirit is the
logical outcome of the classical spirit strengthened by the scientific
spirit. This spirit delights in abstraction, generalizes profusely, and
considers man as a creature apart from his environment, isolated from
his past; it lacks the subtle empiricism which characterizes the English
reformists; it is ignorant of everything touching reality. Accordingly
it sets out to make laws for universal man, without regard for France's
age-old traditions or the local conditions of these provinces. This contention advanced with talent and a semblance of thorough documentation by Taine has beguiled a great number of excellent minds because
of its specious clarity.[3]

These contentions have not stood the test of serious scrutiny by
literary historians trained in more rigid methods since the dawn of
the twentieth century. The penetration with which Gustave Lanson
has laid bare many of our preudices concerning the eighteenth century
forms one of his best-established claims upon our gratitude. Numerous
investigators, Frenchmen and Americans especially, have since followed
upon the path that he had pointed out. Lanson's ideas in their turn
have become accepted opinion and doubtless it will be necessary to

[3] [Taine's celebrated thesis, that in rousing France to revolution the role of
the *philosophes* was both capital and nefarious, is advanced in *Les Origines de la
France contemporaine* (1875–1894).]

modify and complete them in the future by adopting new points of view. It is none the less true that it is thanks to him and to Daniel Mornet after him that we can state today that the three assertions summed up earlier are contradicted by the facts. The French revolution is truly of French origin. If certain foreigners, in particular Locke, whose name may be found at almost all the century's crossroads of ideas, did exert a real influence in France, this influence was assimilated and naturalized there. It had moreover implanted itself in a group of ideas going back to Bayle, Saint-Evremond, Le Vayer, Naudé and Montaigne, which were quite as indigenous and "French" as the absolutism of Bossuet. The philosophical Clubs and similar groups that made themselves felt in France around 1750 and played an active part after 1789 are not all revolutionary—far from it! Furthermore, the part that they played in preparing the Revolution is nowhere clearly ascertained. The role of a gigantic conspiracy attributed by some to Freemasonry is a myth.

Finally and above all, nothing justifies the assertion made with assurance by Taine that the writers of the eighteenth century were men of reason alone with no experience of the realities of life. In their time there was some use of empty rhetoric, as there is in every time; the Revolutionaries for their part will cherish a type of eloquence reminiscent of the ancients, and be occasionally intoxicated with words; they will also have an ambition to proclaim universal truths and formulate principles for all men. It is not certain that this ambition is not one of the finest qualities of the French Revolution. But it would be a mistake to forget that the eighteenth century is a great century in science, as much or more so in experimental science as in deductive and abstract disciplines. The works of M. Mornet have proved that eighteenth-century thinkers were on the contrary suspicious of scholastic generalizations and of systems in general: they made observations and conducted experiments. They introduced into education the taste for very detailed empiricism and for actual practice in the arts and trades. They praised techniques and described them with care. They traveled like Montesquieu in order to see at close hand constitutions and the way people lived by them. They cultivated the soil, in the case of the physiocrats; lived on their lands, as did Helvétius; or administered provinces, like Turgot. The most thoroughgoing Revolutionaries had not, like Marx or Lenin, spent years in reading-rooms; they were petty lawyers in contact with the people, like Robespierre at Arras, veterinaries like Marat; in short, provincial men who knew the lives of the peasant, the artisan and the humble country priest of France. Taine's abstraction existed chiefly in his mind, and perhaps in that of Descartes and in a few works of Rousseau. But the Revolution was hardly Cartesian and never put into practice as a complete doctrine the ideas of the *Contrat Social,* which are moreover as contradictory as they are logical.

II

So let us differ with those who claim a priori that the Revolution sprang from the teachings of the "Philosophes," only in order to justify their condemnation of both the Revolution and the teaching. But in opposition to this group, the admirers of the "Philosophes" and even more the admirers of Rousseau, who was not exactly one of the "Philosophes," have taken up the cudgels in an attempt to deny the responsibility or even the guilt of the eighteenth-century political writers in the upheaval that ensued. Particularly notable among these efforts is Edme Champion's abstruse but well-informed book: *Rousseau et la Révolution française* (Colin, 1909). Bringing the concept of retroactive responsibility into these matters is a questionable method. "My God!" Karl Marx is said to have exclaimed on one of the rare occasions when he seems to have called upon Heaven, "preserve me from the Marxists!" Rousseau has accused himself of enough sins without our taxing his memory with the errors of his followers. Without inquiring whether the Revolution was good or bad, which would be entirely too naïve in this day, may we not be able to show how and in what way it absorbed, reflected or brought to fruition the ideas of thinkers who had prepared it without wishing for it?

Professional historians generally tend to limit the part played by ideas in world events: the best of them devote, apparently for the sake of form, one or two chapters to the literature, painting and music of the periods studied by their manuals. But the history of civilization and culture is still very clumsily related to general history. Historians prefer to emphasize the purely historical causes of the Revolution: financial disorder, ministerial blunders, or the hostility of parlements that had been alienated by encroachments upon their prerogatives, etc. Perhaps in doing so they are choosing the easiest way. Their history does grasp the events, the things that change, that is, the things that would be presented in today's newspapers as facts or news: a tax-measure, a famine, the dismissal of a minister, a change in the price

of bread, or a treaty. But it often fails to apprehend the slow subterranean movements which minds inclined to be too matter-of-fact
find intangible, until they one day make their appearance as acts that
make news or usher in a historical era. Now there are cases in which
they never appear as acts; and orthodox history gives scant consideration to abortive movements or history's side-roads into which the past
has ventured briefly only to turn back.

The history of ideas has the advantage of being able to give leisurely
consideration to elements of history that changed only slowly and did
not necessarily express themselves in events which demand attention
by virtue of their suddenness. It would gladly declare that ideas rule
the world. This would doubtless be an over-optimistic creed, if one
did not add immediately that these ideas often turn into those truths
wrapped in the gilt paper of falsehood that our contemporaries call
in France "mystiques," or that they crystallize into a few fetish-words
which imprison or falsify them. The history of the idea of progress
has been sketched, although insufficiently in our opinion, by J. Del-
vaille and the English writer J. M. Bury. History itself would owe
much to the man who would attempt to write the story of the idea
of evolution, or the idea of revolution, the idea of comfort, or the idea
of efficiency and the myth of success in the United States, among
many others. On occasion he would have to go beyond the texts or
interpret them, but this should not be forbidden provided that it is
done with intellectual honesty. One must also remember the fact that
the history of ideas is not simply the exposition of theoretical views
expressed in philosophical writings, but at the same time the history
of the deformations undergone by these ideas when other men adopt
them, and also the history of the half-conscious beliefs into which
ideas first clearly conceived by the few promptly transform themselves.
In his lectures published in Buenos Aires in 1940 under the title *Ideas
y creencias* the Spanish philosopher Ortega y Gasset had rightly claimed
for these half-formulated "beliefs" a position in historical works on a
par with that of ideas.

The difficulties presented by such a history of ideas when they
become beliefs, articles of faith, or emotional drives and impel men
to action are enormous: they should, by this very fact, challenge re-
search-men. Up to now, sociology has failed to make over the study
of literature to any considerable degree because histories of the prevailing taste and the environment in which a writer lived and of the
social and economic conditions in which he was placed while con-

ceiving his work have little bearing on the creation and even the content of the original work. But a knowledge of the public that greeted a literary work or of the work's subsequent career might on the contrary prove extremely fruitful. Such knowledge requires painstaking inquiry into the work's success, based on a great number of facts; it also demands a qualitative interpretation of history and statistics and the occasional intervention of that much-feared "queen of the world" called imagination. For the most read book is not the one that exerts the greatest influence. A hundred thousand passive or half-attentive readers who bought and even leafed through the *Encyclopédie,* for example, count for less than five hundred passionate admirers of the *Contrat Social* if among the latter may be counted Robespierre, Saint-Just or Babeuf. A school-master or a lecturer heard with interest may pass on Marx or Nietzsche to generations of barely literate people who will never guess the source of a thought that has modified their whole lives. It is not even necessary to have understood a book or even to have read it through in order to be profoundly influenced by it. An isolated phrase quoted in some article or a page reproduced at some time in an anthology, may have done more to spread some of the opinions of Montesquieu, Proudhon, or Gobineau than thirty re-editions of their writings bought by private libraries and commented upon by ten provincial academies.

In 1933 Daniel Mornet published on the subject sketched here his work entitled *Les Origines intellectuelles de la Révolution française* (Colin), which is a study of the spread of ideas justly termed a model of intellectual probity and discretion. Henceforth no one can consider this historical and philosophical problem without owing much to this solid book. The author has avoided the error of so many other writers who make the Revolution inexplicable by drawing a rough contrast between 1789 and 1670 or even 1715. He has followed the slow progress of the spread of new ideas from 1715 to 1747, then from 1748 to 1770, the date when the philosophic spirit had won the day. He has made very searching inquiries into the degree of penetration of the reformist spirit among the more or less learned societies and academies, in the letters of private individuals, in provincial libraries and even in educational curricula. His conclusions are new in many respects because of the exact information they offer and because they show those who are misled by the perspective of a later day into the error of limiting the group of "Philosophes" to five or six names, that writers half-unknown to us (Toussaint, Delisle de Sales, Morellet,

Mably) were among those most widely read in the eighteenth century. With fitting reserve they tend to show that the thought of the century, by itself, would never have caused the Revolution if there had not been misery among the people as well; and that misery which was not a new thing at the time would not have brought about the Revolution if it had not had the support of opinion that had long been discontented and desirous of reform. It is clear that the Revolution had various causes including historical causes, meaning economic, political and financial causes as well as intellectual ones. However it would seem that Mornet has limited the role of the latter causes to an excessive degree and further work still needs to be done after his admirable effort.[4]

The most obvious justification for further research lies in the fact that his investigation leaves off at 1787 because of the very purpose of his work. Now if a revolution was ready to break out at the time of the preparation of the "Cahiers de doléances" for the States-General it was not the Revolution that actually developed. Neither the days of June 20th and August 10th 1792, nor the death of Louis XVI nor the Terror, nor the constructive work of the Convention was contained in germ in the convocation of the States-General. In fact we know very little about the influence of Montesquieu, Voltaire and Rousseau himself on the different phases of the Revolution or the way in which they influenced certain actors in the great drama.

The special quality of the French Revolution, compared with other revolutionary movements in France or other countries, obviously lies in the titanic proportions of this upheaval but also in an ardent passion for thought, for embodying ideas in deeds, and for proposing universal laws. This accounts for the unparalleled world-wide influence of the work of destruction and construction which was accomplished between 1789 and 1795. An abstract passion for justice and liberty, the latter being sometimes conceived in strange fashion, inspired the men who made the Revolution and those who prepared it. The original tone that characterizes the Revolution and the verve that enlivens it, which are fundamental things although they elude the grasp of facts and figures, are due in part to the movement of thought and sensibility

[4] [While Peyre's statement is in the main correct, it perhaps does not do full justice to the evolution of Mornet's views. By the time he wrote Les Origines, his last word on the subject, he had come to the conclusion that the Revolution was inexplicable without reference to the philosophes who awakened the intelligence of the middle classes and gave them ideas with which to fight the establishment.]

which goes from Montesquieu to Rousseau and from Bayle to the abbé Raynal.

III

If there is really one almost undisputed conclusion on the origins of the Revolution reached by historical studies coming from radically opposite factions, it is that pure historical materialism does not explain the Revolution. Certainly riots due to hunger were numerous in the eighteenth century and Mornet draws up the list of them; there was discontent and agitation among the masses. But such had also been the case under Louis XIV, such was the case under Louis-Philippe and deep discontent existed in France in 1920 and 1927 and 1934 without ending in revolution. No great event in history has been due to causes chiefly economic in nature and certainly not the French Revolution. France was not happy in 1788, but she was happier than the other countries of Europe and enjoyed veritable economic prosperity. Her population had increased from 19 to 27 millions since the beginning of the century and was the most numerous in Europe. French roads and bridges were a source of admiration to foreigners. Her industries such as ship-fitting at Bordeaux, the silk-industry at Lyons and the textile-industry at Rouen, Sedan and Amiens were active while Dietrich's blast furnaces and the Creusot were beginning to develop modern techniques in metallurgy. The peasants were little by little coming to be owners of the land. Foreign trade reached the sum of 1,153 million francs in 1787, a figure not to be attained again until 1825. The traffic in colonial spices and San Domingo sugar was a source of wealth. Banks were being founded and France owned half the specie existing in Europe. So misery in France was no more than relative. But truly wretched people such as the Egyptian fellah, the pariah of India or even the Balkan or Polish peasant or Bolivian miners for example rarely bring about revolutions. In order to revolt against one's lot, one must be aware of his wretched condition, which presupposes a certain intellectual and cultural level; one must have a clear conception of certain reforms that one would like to adopt; in short, one must be convinced (and it was on this point that the books of the eighteenth century produced their effect) that things are not going well, that they might be better and that they will be better if the measures proposed by the reformist thinkers are put into practice.

Eighteenth-century philosophy taught the Frenchman to find his condition wretched, or in any case, unjust and illogical and made him disinclined to the patient resignation to his troubles that had long characterized his ancestors. It had never called for a revolution nor desired a change of regime; it had never been republican and Camille Desmoulins was not wrong in stating: "In all France there were not ten of us who were republicans before 1789." Furthermore he himself was not one of those ten. But only an over-simplified conception of influence would indulge in the notion that political upheaval completely embodies in reality the theoretical design drawn up by some thinker. Even the Russian revolution imbued as it was with Marxian dialectic did not make a coherent application of Marxism or quickly found it inapplicable when tried. The reforms of limited scope advocated by *L'Esprit des Lois, L'Homme aux quarante écus, L'Encyclopédie* and the more moderate writings of Rousseau struck none the less deeply at the foundations of the *ancien régime,* for they accustomed the Frenchman of the Third Estate to declaring privileges unjust, to finding the crying differences between the provinces illogical and finding famines outrageous. The propaganda of the "Philosophes" perhaps more than any other factor accounted for the fulfillment of the preliminary condition of the French revolution, namely, discontent with the existing state of things.

In short, without enlarging upon what is already rather well known we may say that eighteenth-century writers prepared the way for the Revolution, without wishing for it, because:

(a) They weakened the traditional religion, winning over to their side a great number of clerics, and taught disrespect for an institution which had been the ally of the monarchy for hundreds of years. At the same time they had increased the impatience of the non-privileged groups by uprooting from many minds the faith in a future life which had formerly made bearable the sojourn in this vale of tears that constituted life for many people of low estate. They wished to enjoy real advantages here on earth and without delay. The concept of well-being and then that of comfort slowly penetrated among them.

(b) They taught a secular code of ethics, divorced from religious belief and independent of dogma, and made the idea of conduct consist of observation of this system of ethics, which was presented as varying in accordance with climate and environment. Furthermore they gave first importance in this ethical code to the love of humanity, altruism and service due society or our fellowmen. The ideas of humanity, already present in the teaching of Christ, in Seneca and Montaigne but often dormant, suddenly exert fresh influence over people's minds.

(c) They developed the critical spirit and the spirit of analysis and taught many men not to believe, or to suspend judgment rather than accept routine traditions. In D'Argenson, Chamfort, Morelly, Diderot, Voltaire of course, D'Holbach, Condillac and many others, and even in Laclos and Sade, we will find the effort to think courageously without regard for convention or tradition, that will henceforth characterize the French intellectual attitude. From this time on, inequality with respect to taxation, the tithe paid to the Church, and banishment or persecution for subversive opinions will shock profoundly the sense of logic and critical spirit of the readers of the "Philosophes."

(d) Lastly, these very thinkers who have often been depicted as builders of Utopias are the creators of history or the historical sense, or almost so. Montesquieu studiously examined the origins of law and constitutions and saw men "conditioned" by soil and climate in contrast with the absolute rationalists who were foreign jurists and not Frenchmen. Boulainvilliers and many others of lesser fame studied France's past. Voltaire's masterpiece is probably his work on general history. The result of this curiosity about history was two-fold: it encouraged faith in progress and convinced numbers of Frenchmen that it was their task to fulfill humanity's law, to endeavor to increase the sum of liberty, relative equality, "enlightenment" and happiness in the world; it also proved to many men of the law who examined old documents and the titles of nobility and property, that the privileges of nobility were based on a flimsy foundation. The respect that these bourgeois or sons of the people might have felt for the aristocrats was accordingly diminished, at the very moment when the bourgeois saw the nobles not only accept with admiration but take under their protection destructive writings produced by the pens of commoners: sons of tailors (Marmontel), vine-growers (Restif), cutlers (Diderot) and watch-makers (Rousseau). And the history of the origins of royal sovereignty itself seemed to them scarcely more edifying than that of the feudal privileges.

As for the means of dissemination of those ideas or new beliefs that the "Philosophes" were spreading between the years 1715 and 1770 or 1789, it will suffice to enumerate them rapidly, for numerous studies have examined them: they were the salons, although very few of the future revolutionaries frequented society gatherings; the clubs, that more and more called for tolerance, preached deism, demanded the abolition of slavery (*Société des Amis des Noirs*) and dreamed of imitating the American Revolution (*Club Américain*); books or tracts which made their appearance as works of small format, easily carried or hidden, lively and sharp in style and prone to surprise and arouse the reader; periodicals; the theatre especially after the coming of the "drame bourgeois" and the "comédie larmoyante," and then with Beaumarchais; and the education given in the secondary schools. Mornet's book sums up the essential material on the subject that can be found in documents. The other means of spreading new ideas, such as conversation, which is doubtless the most effective means man has always used to borrow and pass on new views, elude documentary research.

It is among the actors in the great revolutionary drama that investigations of broader scope might show us which of the ideas of the eighteenth century exerted influence and how and why they did so. Siéyès, among others, has been the subject of an exhaustive intellectual biography which has established with precision what the young abbé coming to Paris from Fréjus to devise constitutions owed to Descartes, Locke, and Voltaire in particular (for the negative side of his ideas), to Rousseau (for his impassioned logic) and to Mably. (Paul Bastid, *Siéyès et sa pensée*, Hachette, 1939.) Another recent book, by Gérard Walter, is a study of Babeuf (Payot, 1937). It would be instructive to know how the minds of many of the revolutionaries were developed and by what books and meditations they were influenced; such men range from Mirabeau and Danton to Marat, from Rabaut de Saint-Etienne to Hérault de Séchelles and from Desmoulins or Brissot to generals of the Convention who may have read Raynal and Rousseau with passionate interest, as Bonaparte did later. Only when many monographs have been written devoting at least as much if not more attention to the history of ideas and the psychology of the protagonists in the Revolution than to the facts of their lives of action, will we be able to make sure generalizations about the influence of Montesquieu or Rousseau on the France of '89 or '93.

IV

Montesquieu and Rousseau are certainly the two great names worthy of consideration in some detail. The presiding judge of the High Court of Bordeaux obviously did not want the Revolution; had he lived to see it, he would not have approved of its reorganization of the judiciary, nor its audacity in reform, nor the Declaration of the Rights of Man, nor even the interpretation of certain principles he himself had enunciated. Still he is one of the spiritual fathers of the first two revolutionary assemblies. Like so many other men who have made history, he influenced the fateful years of 1789–92 by what he did say almost involuntarily, by the thoughts other men read in his sentences and by the tone even more than by the content of his writings. His great work [5] breathes a veritable hatred of despotism founded on fear; it shows no moral respect for monarchy, and so helped to alienate the most reasonable minds from it. The great principle of the separation of powers presumes the right to seize from the king the united powers that he believed he held as a whole by divine right. Finally, Montesquieu, however elevated his position as a citizen or as a magistrate may have been, uttered words which will assume a mystic authority in later times on the subject of the people's inherent good qualities and its ability to select its leaders: "The common people are admirable in choosing those to whom they must delegate some part of their authority," (II,ii) or "When the common people once have sound principles, they adhere to them longer than those we are wont to call respectable people. Rarely does corruption have its beginning among the people." (V,ii)

Finally, in his admirable XIth book, Montesquieu had defined liberty in terms that were to remain etched in people's memories: this liberty required stable laws, which alone could establish and protect it. These laws were also to correct economic inequality. Certainly its historical examples adduced in great profusion, highly technical juridical considerations, certain generalizations that had been too cleverly made symmetrical and its lack of order made this voluminous treatise hard to read. But Montesquieu's influence was not one of those that can be gauged by the number of readers: it expressed itself in action thanks to a few thoughtful minds who found in it a sufficiently coherent overall plan capable of replacing the old order which obviously was crumbling. Montesquieu's influence inspired a more important group of revolutionaries who were familiar with only a few chapters of his work, but these chapters were filled with the love of freedom and the great feeling for humanity that condemned slavery and the iniquitous exploitation of some men by others.

Montesquieu's influence on the French Revolution began to decline at the time when Rousseau's was coming to the fore. Many studies have been devoted to the subject of Rousseau and the French Revolution; and the subject deserves still further study, for perhaps

[5] [The *Esprit des lois* (1748).]

no more notable case of the effect of thought on life exists in the whole history of ideas and of dynamic ideas in particular. But this broad subject has too often been narrowed down by the most well-meaning historians. So many dogmatic and partisan statements had portrayed Rousseau as the great malefactor who was guilty of the excesses committed by the Terrorists and as the father of collectivism that, as a reaction, the best-disposed scholars set about proving by facts and texts that the author of the *Contrat Social* was guiltless of so many misdeeds. As a result they have belittled his influence. But there is some narrowness and naïveté in these scholarly arguments.

According to some, everything that Rousseau wrote already existed before his coming in the works of a number of writers and thinkers both at home and abroad and Jean-Jacques brought forth very little that was new. That is quite possible, and scholars have been able to make fruitful inquiries into the sources of the *Discours sur l'Inégalité* and the *Contrat*. But the fact remains that whatever Rousseau borrowed from others he made his own; he rethought it and above all felt it with a new intensity and set it off to advantage by his own passion and his own talent. What he owes to Plato or Locke suddenly "shook" the men of 1792 only because Rousseau had charged it with a new electric current.

Furthermore Rousseau is rife with contradictions and the most ingenious men of learning (Lanson, Höffding, Schinz and E. H. Wright) have not yet succeeded in convincing us of the unity of his thought. For Corsica and Poland he proposes finely adapted and moderate constitutions that do not seem to have sprung from the same brain as the *Contrat Social*. He writes a very conservative article on *l'Economie politique* for the fifth volume of the *Encyclopédie* while in his second *Discours* he had propounded anarchical theses burning with revolutionary ardor. "To expect one to be always consistent is beyond human possibility, I fear!" he himself had admitted in the second preface of the *Nouvelle Héloïse*. We will not go so far as to pay homage to Rousseau for his contradictions and may choose to reserve our unalloyed admiration for other systems of thought more dispassionate and logical than his. But an author's influence does not have much to do with the rigor and coherence of his philosophical system. In fact, it would not be hard to show that the thinkers who have contributed the most toward changing the face of the world exerted influence because of their contradictions, since very different periods and highly diverse individuals drew from them various messages of equal validity. Let us add with no ironic intention that because of this the ingenuity of the learned will never tire of seeking the impossible golden key to these disconcerting enigmas and that the hunger for systems, among those lacking the necessary imagination to construct new ones, will always exert itself to bring about a happy synthesis of the successive assertions of a Plato, a Montaigne, a Locke, Rousseau, Comte or Nietzsche.

After all, as the historians tell us quite correctly, the *Contrat Social* is only a part of Rousseau's political thought and not the most important part in the eyes of his contemporaries; the author himself attributed only a rather limited importance to this logical Utopian book. Rousseau never seriously contemplated a revolution in France; he did not think that a republic was viable, or perhaps even desirable for France. One might even make the assertion supported by texts that Jean-Jacques, that *bête noire* of the anti-revolutionaries from Burke to Maurras, Lasserre and Seillière, was a timid conservative. It is quite true (M. Mornet has proved this once again) that the influence of the *Contrat Social* was very weak between the years 1762 and 1789; the book caused so little disturbance that Rousseau was not even molested; and it is probable that Rousseau would have been frightened by certain inferences that were later drawn from his ideas. What he wrote in 1765 in no way justifies an assertion on our part that he would still have written the same thing in 1793 and so it is quite as conceivable that Rousseau might have violently changed his point of view and espoused the cause of the revolutionaries, had he lived long enough to receive their acclaim. And above all, without having consciously wanted the Revolution, Rousseau did a great deal, if not to cause it, at least to give it direction when it had broken out. The success of Rousseau's works and the reception accorded them in his life-time have been investigated in sufficient detail. From now on groups of research men might well give their attention to the enormous influence Rousseau exerted on the men of the Convention and on those of the Empire or the Restoration or on the Romantics. Granted that Rousseau was neither a republican nor a revolutionary, he was in revolt and that is no less important. A. Aulard who was not inclined to over-estimate the influence of the intellectuals on the French Revolution nevertheless accurately described the paradoxical result of any fairly broad study of this subject: "All these men in revolt want to keep the monarchy and all of them blindly deal it mortal blows. The French, monarchists to a man, take on republicanism without their knowledge."

Not one of the men of the Revolution adopted Rousseau's philosophical system outright in order to put it into practice; that is only too plain. Not one of them understood Rousseau's thought in its subleties, its contradictions and its alterations as the scholar of the present-day can undrestand it with the aid of much posthumous documentation: this is scarcely less obvious. Whatever chagrin it may cause minds devoted to strict methods, the unparalleled effect produced on the imagination of posterity by Montaigne, Rousseau or Nietzsche can be credited to quotations drawn from their contexts and probably perverted from their original sense. This influence is not so much an influence of ideas as it is an influence of *idées-forces,* to use Fouillée's expression, and exerts its power more by setting men's sensibilities aflame than by convincing their minds.

"Man is born free, and everywhere he is in chains." This peremptory formula from the first chapter of the *Contrat Social,* in conjunction with a few others which declared the sovereignty of the people inalienable and affirmed the right to revolt in the event of the usurpation of powers by the government, contributed immeasurably toward crystallizing in the general mind from 1789 on the resolve to make the king subject to the only true rights which were inherent in the people. On October 5th 1789 Robespierre and Barrère contended that the sovereign could not oppose the constituent power which was superior to him. The passion for equality which wildly inspires the Revolutionaries and the modern world after them owes no less to Rousseau's fundamental idea that law should rectify natural inequality (which he was not foolish enough to overlook) by means of civic equality. The XIth chapter of the 2nd book of the *Contrat Social* stated in striking terms: "For the very reason that the force of things always tends to destroy equality, the force of legislation must always tend to maintain it." The 3rd book of the same work castigated the vices to which kings are prone, for if they are not narrow or evil on attaining the throne—"the throne will make them so." That does not make Rousseau a partisan of republicanism or a democrat; but had it not been for such aphorisms, Saint-Just never would have proclaimed in his fine *Discours concernant le jugement de Louis XVI* of November 13 1792: "Royalty is an eternal crime against which every man has the right to rise up and take arms. . . . One can not reign in innocence."

The *Discours sur l'Inégalité* contained pages of impassioned rhetoric that were even more effective. The English writer C. E. Vaughan, who is a scrupulous commentator on the political writings of Rousseau, did not hesitate to state, after years of reflection on this subject: "Wherever, during the last century and a half, man has revolted against injustice and oppression, there we may be sure that the leaven of the second *Discourse* has been working." Doubtless Rousseau had never dreamed of the application of his declamations against property; but he had set forth the idea that inheritances ought to be whittled down by fiscal measures and that those who owned no lands ought to receive some, without necessarily advocating collectivism. He had also uttered against wealth words whose echoes will ring down the centuries: "It is the estate of the wealthy that steals from mine the bread of my children. . . . A bond-holder whom the State pays for doing nothing is scarcely different in my eyes from a highwayman who lives at the expense of the passers-by . . . , every idle citizen is a rogue."

The precautions with which Jean-Jacques had surrounded some of his bold affirmations quickly disappeared in the heat of action. The chapter called "Du Peuple," in the *Contrat Social* (ii, 8), was most cautious: but its author had nevertheless hinted in it that sometimes, in the life of peoples, "the State, set aflame by civil wars, is so to speak reborn from its ashes, and regains the vigor of youth in leaving the arms of death." People retained phrases from the *Emile* too,—the prophetic phrases in which the educator had proclaimed to the people of his time that they were approaching the era of revolutions when men would be able to destroy what men had built. These few phrases, gaining added violence in tone from the fact that they were detached from contexts that often contradicted them, seemed charged with new meaning when the great upheaval had broken out. Such was also the case of the mystic system of happiness taught by the Genevan "philosophe's" entire work. Man is born good; he is made to be happy; he may become so if he reforms himself and if his governments are reformed. We know how the echo of these doctrines will resound in the noble formulas of Saint-Just, who was perhaps the revolutionary most deeply steeped in Rousseau's thought.

The aspect of Rousseau that Albert Schinz called "the Roman Rousseau" exerted no less influence on that other myth which prevailed or raged among the men of the Revolution (and among the women, too, as in the case of Madame Rolland), the myth of the ancients and their passion for liberty and virtue. "The world has been empty since the day of the Romans," cried Saint-Just; and he stated to the Convention on February 24th 1793: "The Republic is not a Senate, it is virtue." The whole of Saint-Just's remarkable youthful work entitled *Esprit de la Révolution et de la Constitution de la France* is imbued with Rousseauist themes and ends on this cry of regret: "France has only now conferred a statue upon J.-J. Rousseau. Ah! Why is that great man dead?"

Robespierre, whom Michelet maliciously called a "weak and pale bastard of Rousseau" because of his cult of the Supreme Being, was indebted to Rousseau to no lesser degree than Saint-Just, although he does not show the mark of the born writer that stamps the formulas of the terrorist guillotined at the age of twenty-seven. It was by assiduous reading of Rousseau that he formed his style: and his style served him as a powerful weapon. It seems that the young student from Arras met Rousseau in 1778, the year of his death, and never forgot it. "I saw thee in thy last days, and this memory is a source of proud joy for me," he declares later in his *Mémoires,* placed under the aegis of Rousseau, and promised to "remain constantly faithful to the inspiration that I have drawn from thy writings." Dozens of sentences which reiterate formulas from the *Contrat Social* might be extracted from his speeches. It was Rousseau who had helped to turn Robespierre away from Catholicism, and of course he was the man from whom Robespierre borrowed his cult of the Supreme Being; his *Observations sur le projet d'Instruction publique* presented to the Convention in 1793 are based on the Rousseauist faith: "If nature created man good, it is back to nature that we must bring him." His speech made at the Jacobin Club on January 2nd 1792 against the war at that time desired by the Girondins rendered homage to Rousseau in impassioned terms: "No one has given us a more exact idea of the common people than Rousseau because no one loved them more." The secret of the enormous influence exerted by Rousseau lay less in the substance of his thought than in the burning tone of a man who had lived his ideas and had suffered (or thought he had) because he had sprung from the people and had known poverty. "According to the principles of your committee," declared Robespierre to the Constituent Assembly on August 11, 1791, "we ought to blush at having erected a statue to J.-J. Rousseau, because he did not pay the property-tax." The history of ideas and their influence on persons and things is full of elements that defy all possibility of quantitative or statistical measurement. How can one estimate all that the men of the Revolution owed Rousseau in the way of fervor, mystic hope, logic that was impassioned and even fierce on occasion and–

what is not less important, even for history, as Danton, Saint-Just and
Robespierre were aware—the imperious and incisive style that made their
formulas resound in twenty countries and across one hundred and
fifty years? "One does not make revolutions by halves" or "the French
people are voting for liberty for the world"—these aphorisms or decrees
of Saint-Just, like certain phrases of Mirabeau, or a multitude of
orators of lesser stature, and of Bonaparte himself, would not have been
uttered, and would not have had the resonance that has kept them
alive, if these men had not been imbued with the spirit and the style of
the Citizen of Geneva.

The history of the cult of Rousseau during the French Revolution
is easier to trace than that of his deep influence on the revolutionaries.
The former has been studied in part, and the manifestations of this
idolatry of Rousseau are often amusing. The setting-up of the bust of
Jean-Jacques in the Constituent Assembly on June 23, 1790, the con-
secration of a street of Paris named after him in the same year, the
repeated editions of the *Contrat Social* (4 editions in 1790, 3 in 1791,
etc.), the constitutional articles put under his aegis, the decree ordering
that Rousseau's ashes be brought to the Pantheon in 1794 and the pious
emotion of the crowd, and lastly, the invocation to "his generous soul"
by the Incorruptible One in his speech of May 7th 1794 on the religion
of the Revolution and the pompous application of his declamations on
the Supreme Being; all these things have been mentioned more than
once and recently, too.[6] But the way in which Rousseau's influence
profoundly modified the men and women of the revolutionary and
imperial era, and then the romantics great and small, and the contin-
uators of the Revolution, in and out of France, in the nineteenth and
twentieth centuries: these are the questions that intellectual history
seems to have been reluctant to investigate.

Its timidity is regrettable and our knowledge of the past suffers
twice over because of it: first, because history that devotes itself too exclusively to what we call material facts such as a military victory, the
fall of a ministry or the opening-up of a railroad-track, seriously falsifies
our perspective of what took place. The development of the Napoleonic
legend, the quietly working influence of Rousseau or Voltaire, the
growth of anticlericalism and the elaboration of socialist myths are
phenomena which are partly literary or sentimental in nature, but are
second to no other order of phenomena in importance and in the effects

[6] See Gordon McNeil: "The Cult of Rousseau in the French Revolution,"
Journal of the History of Ideas, April 1945, 196–212.

they had on the course of human affairs. Our knowledge of the past suffers additionally because historians, by turning aside from the history of ideas and sentiments with their vigorous influence on the lives of men, abandon these research subjects to men less trained than themselves in exact methods of study; the latter are disposed to write with the sole intent of finding in the past arguments to support their political views or their partisan claims. Meanwhile youth is tempted to reject history as it is officially presented, as an endless series of wars, diplomatic ruses, crimes, examples of intense selfishness and the impotent efforts of men to bring more reason into the world. It refuses to lend credence to those who advise it that man has remained a religious and ideological animal even more than an "economic" creature. Youth's awakening, when it is suddenly placed face to face with the terrible power of ideas, myths and fanaticisms in the world, is sometimes a rude shock, as we have seen recently.

The Frenchmen in particular who have thought fit in the past few years to deny their eighteenth-century thinkers as traitors to the classic and monarchical tradition of France have only to open their eyes in order to ascertain that no French tradition is more alive than that of the Century of Enlightenment. Pascal and Descartes are doubtless greater; Montaigne has more charm and Saint Thomas more logical power: but it is Voltaire and Rousseau, and sometimes Montesquieu and Condorcet, that one finds almost always behind the living influence of France on the masses and the ideologies of South America, of the United States itself, of central and eastern Europe and that one will find tomorrow in Africa and Asia. The world of today expects from post-war France, and France herself expects from her political thinkers who had lost the habit of expressing themselves in universal terms during the last fifty years, a renewal and a modernization of her liberal ideas of the eighteenth century, boldly adapted to the social and economic problems of today, but still inspired by the same faith in man and his possibilities.

Students from other countries remind the French of this fact, lest they forget it too readily. Their studies on the influence of Voltaire and Rousseau on the French Revolution and the revolutions that ensued elsewhere in the world are becoming more numerous and sometimes more objective than the French ones. A Slavic scholar Milan Markovitch in a large and exhaustive book on *Rousseau et Tolstoi* (Champion, 1928) set forth in detail the Rousseauism of the Russian novelist, who in his adolescence carried the portrait of Jean-Jacques around his neck

like a scapular and wrote the following message to the newly-founded
Rousseau Club on March 7th 1905: "Rousseau has been my teacher
since the age of fifteen. Rousseau and the Gospel have been the two
great influences for good in my life." The German thinker Ernst Cassirer devoted a little book written in 1945 to commemoration of the
admiration for Rousseau expressed by Goethe and Fichte as well as
Kant who declared: "Rousseau set me right. . . . I learned to respect
human nature." Thoreau and D. H. Lawrence are indebted to the
Genevan for a good half of their thinking. George Eliot, on meeting the
philosopher Emerson in Coventry in 1848, found herself being asked by
him what her favorite book was; Rousseau's *Confessions,* she answered;
at which the American transcendentalist cried: "It is mine too." Shortly
afterwards, on February 9th 1849, she wrote Sara Hennel these extremely lucid sentences on the mechanism of intellectual influence:

I wish you thoroughly to understand that the writers who have most
profoundly influenced me are not in the least oracles to me. . . . For
instance, it would signify nothing to me if a very wise person were to stun
me with proofs that Rousseau's views of life, religion, and government
were miserably erroneous,—that he was guilty of some of the worst *bassesses*
that have degraded civilized man. I might admit all this: and it would be
not the less true that Rousseau's genius has sent that electric thrill through
my intellectual and moral frame which has awakened me to new perceptions;
. . . and this not by teaching me any new belief. . . . The fire of his
genius has so fused together old thoughts and prejudices, that I have been
ready to make new combinations.

In the face of such proofs of a fruitful and life-giving though possibly dangerous influence, an important English historian who was
moreover an admirer of Burke and usually more moderate in his statements, but was conscious of the importance of ideas in the events of
this world, Lord Acton, was impelled to exclaim: "Rousseau produced
more effect with his pen than Aristotle, or Cicero, or St. Augustine, or
St. Thomas Acquinas, or any other man who ever lived."

THE MEANING OF ROMANTICISM FOR THE HISTORIAN OF IDEAS *

Arthur O. Lovejoy †

The editor has omitted the first three pages of this essay in which the author discusses the signification of the two leading words in the title, namely "meaning" and "Romanticism." Apropos of the latter, Lovejoy reiterates his well-known thesis, developed in a number of previous articles, that "Romanticism" does not have one accepted meaning but on the contrary "an amazing diversity of meanings."

Nothing, then, but confusion and error can result from the quest of some supposititious intrinsic nature of a hypostatized essence called "Romanticism." [1] But there is a quite different sort of inquiry into which our initial question may be converted; and such an inquiry would make for the elimination of confusion, and is indispensable for the understanding of the history of the past century and a half, and, consequently, for the understanding of the contemporary intellectual, moral and political situation; and this inquiry is primarily the business of the historian of ideas, and requires the application of a specific method of analysis proper to that study. Its starting-point is a massive historical fact which no one is likely to deny—namely, that in the last quarter of the eighteenth century, especially in the 1780s and 1790s, there were discovered, invented or revived, chiefly in Germany, a large number of ideas which

---

* Reprinted from the *Journal of the History of Ideas*, June 1941, pp. 260–278. Copyright 1941 by the *Journal of the History of Ideas*. Used by permission of the *Journal of the History of Ideas*.

† Arthur O. Lovejoy was Professor of Philosophy at Johns Hopkins University from 1910 to 1938. Among his many publications in the history of ideas are *The Great Chain of Being* and *Essays in the History of Ideas*.

[1] [The following books are recommended for an introduction to Romanticism in general: Irving Babbitt, *Rousseau and Romanticism* (Boston: Houghton Mifflin, 1919); Jacques Barzun, *Romanticism and the Modern Ego* (Boston: Little, Brown,1943); L. A. Willoughby, *The Romantic Movement in Germany* (London: Oxford University Press, 1930); Sir Maurice Bowra, *The Romantic Imagination* (Cambridge: Harvard University Press, 1949); Arthur O. Lovejoy, *Essays in the History of Ideas* (Baltimore: Johns Hopkins University Press, 1948). The last is especially important for discriminating among the different types of Romanticism.]

had been relatively, though not always absolutely, unfamiliar or un
influential through most of the seventeenth and eighteenth centuries; [2]
and that the total impact of what we may call, for short, the new ideas
of the 1780s and 1790s (including revivals of old ideas under "new"),
as they developed, ramified, and were diffused during the following
decades, profoundly altered the habitual preconceptions, valuations,
and ruling catchwords of an increasingly large part of the educated
classes in Europe, so that there came into vogue in the course of the
nineteenth century and in our own a whole series of intellectual
fashions—from styles in poetry and styles in metaphysics to styles in
government—which had no parallels in the preceding period. The
result was—to resort to the hackneyed but apt metaphor—not one, but a
whole set of "climates of opinion," in which species of plants either
unknown to the earlier eighteenth century or only germinant then,
came to flourish mightily. The "newness" of these ideas of (e.g.) the
1790s was, for the most part, not an absolute newness; it lies in the
contrast with the dominant ideas of the immediately antecedent age,
and with what may be called the "old ideas" of the 1790s, exemplified,
on the political side, in the French Revolution. For, roughly, in that
decade two revolutions were taking place—one, external and political,
in France, which was the culmination of the *Aufklärung*, the other,
primarily in the realm of abstract ideas, mainly in Germany,[3] which
was only somewhat later to manifest its political consequences—some of
them, indeed, only in our own unhappy day.

To call these new ideas of the 1780s and 1790s "Romanticism" is
confusion-breeding and productive of historical error above all because
it suggests that there was only one such idea, or, if many, that they
were all implicates of one fundamental "Romantic" idea, or, at the
least, that they were harmonious *inter se* and formed a sort of systematic
unity. None of these things are true. The new ideas of the period—
even when held, as they often were, by the same individual minds—
were in large part heterogeneous, logically independent, and sometimes
essentially antithetic to one another in their implications, though their

[2] [On pre-Romanticism—that is, Romanticism prior to the outburst of the late
eighteenth century—see, in addition to Lovejoy's *Essays*, Paul Hazard, *European
Thought in the Eighteenth Century* (New Haven: Yale University Press, 1954),
pp. 353–393; and Kenneth Clark, *The Gothic Revival* (London: Constable &
Co., 1928).]

[3] [John Herman Randall, Jr., *The Making of the Modern Mind* (Boston:
Houghton Mifflin, rev. ed., 1940), pp. 389–427, is particularly good on the
opposition between the Enlightenment and the new ideas.]

full implications were not always at once discerned; and some writers traditionally labelled "Romantic" were influenced by some of them, others by others, and yet others, I suspect, by none. But though there is no such thing as Romanticism, there emphatically *was* something which—for lack of any other brief name—may still be called a Romantic period; and one may perhaps speak of—not a, but several, Romantic movements: the period in which this array of new or newly energized ideas emerged into prominence, and the movements which consist in the propagation of one or many of them, in the drawing out of their initially latent consequences, logical or pseudological, in their alliances with one another or with various older ideas and fashions of thought, and in their interaction with certain more or less permanent affective elements of human nature. For my own part, at any rate, I am—in a spirit of compromise—willing to speak of such a period and of such movements—meaning, approximately, the half-century 1780–1830, but especially its second decade, and the movements in which any one or more of these ideas conspicuously manifested themselves. In what follows I shall be chiefly concerned with some of the ideas of those German writers who, in the 1790s, first introduced the *term* "Romantic" as the designation of a new tendency or fashion of thought.

Now the question: What were the new, or newly *active* and peculiarly influential, ideas of the 1790s and what were their vicissitudes and developments in the subsequent decades? is a factual and therefore a properly historical question. But it is a question in the history of ideas; and it therefore, as I have said, requires the application of a method of investigation appropriate to that study. And the nature of this method, as applied, not to the life-history of a particular idea but to the integral study of a period, still appears to need some explanation. Given the prerequisite knowledge of the relevant texts the first task of the historiographer of ideas is a task of logical analysis—the discrimination *in* the texts, and the segregating *out* of the texts, of each of what I shall call the basic or germinal ideas, the identification of each of them so that it can be recognized wherever it appears, in differing contexts, under different labels or phrasings, and in diverse provinces of thought. And in this part of the task the historian—unhappily—must usually begin by carefully scrutinizing the most recurrent and crucial terms in his texts—the most prevalent formulas or phrases or sacred words—in order to determine what and how many distinct ideas appear to be expressed by, or associated with, each of these terms in the minds of the various users of it. For once a word or phrase or theorem has gained vogue and sanctity, it is likely to be used by different writers in quite different senses—usually without their being clearly aware that they are doing so.

For example: it is, I suppose, commonly recognized that *one* of the relatively new phenomena of the Romantic period was a new or, at all events, a much wider and intensified, vogue of the highly abstract and equivocal term "infinite." It is notorious that such phrases as *Streben ins Unendliche* or *Sehnsucht nach dem Unendlichen* or *Annäherung zu einer unendlichen Grösse,* were peculiarly dear to the German *Frühromantiker* as expressions of their ideal of life or of art. But, as I have elsewhere pointed out, the term "infinite," as used by one or another of these writers, had at least five distinct, though not in all cases mutually exclusive, senses or applications. All of these senses obviously had something in common, and that something was, historically, highly important. The common element was the negative element. The "infinite," whatever positive meaning might be connected with the word, meant at least the not-limited or not-completed, the *Unbegrenzt* or *Unvollendet*—in *some* sense of limit or completion. And the sanctity of the word in most of the new writers of the period was evidence of a tendency to a new presupposition about what is excellent or valuable —and also about the nature of things, the constitution of the universe or the course of history. It was a presupposition contrary to a feature of what may be fairly called the main—not the only—earlier tradition of European thought, at least in value-judgments of all kinds, and not in these alone. There were important opposing strains in the older tradition, but the most prevalent and orthodox tendency had been to think in terms of finites, and to regard limitation as an essential element of excellence, at least for mortals. In logic and science, the first thing needful was to have precisely *defined* concepts and terms; in a work of art, the first essential was that it should have one limited theme and a clear-cut and readily recognizable "form," so that, as Schiller declared in the essay that gave the decisive initial impetus to the early Romantic movement in Germany, the essence of classical art is that it is a *Kunst der Begrenztheit;* in literary style, the supreme merit was the clarity that comes from using words which immediately convey clear and distinct ideas, express exact and therefore limited meanings; and in human character and conduct, the mark of excellence was to observe metes and bounds and to be moderate in all one's desires, ambitions and pretensions. The historic process, too, in the Christian tradition—in spite of opposing Aristotelian and other influences—was conceived as a finite thing, having a beginning, a middle and an end—neither an interminable undulation, nor an endless recurrence of similar cycles, nor even a perpetual movement towards an infinitely distant and therefore unattainable goal. Now the German Romantics of the 1790s were in conscious and zealous—though not in consistent or unwavering—revolt against all assumptions, but first of all in the theory of art. They conceived and proclaimed themselves to be the prophets of a new, a "modern," art—and "modern" is what *they* primarily meant by "Romantic"—which should be a *Kunst des Unendlichen*. The new valuation, the revolt against "the infinite," speedily passed over into other provinces; and since one of the most pregnant differences of taste or habit in categories is that between a habitual preference for the limited and well-defined and a habitual preference for "the infinite," this one among the ideas of the 1790s has had many and far-reaching consequences.

But in spite of this common element in the new vogue of the word "infinite," when any more positive and concrete significations were attached to it by German writers of the 1790s, it could serve as the catchword for several quite distinct and, in part, mutually antagonistic tendencies, since there are numerous varieties of "the infinite." These, again, I may not take the time to enumerate; I merely recall the general fact in order to illustrate the indispensability of a careful semasiological analysis in the first phase of the intellectual historian's study of a period.

When this phase is completed—when he has discriminated and listed as exhaustively as he can the separate "ruling ideas" which distinguish the period, or the particular group of writers in it with whom he is concerned, his next task is to examine the relations between these ideas. And the relations he will need to look for are of three kinds: logical, psychological, and historical—and especially, under the latter, genetic—relations.

The first two of these inquiries I have distinguished from the strictly historical because they are procedures of analysis and construction which need in some measure to be carried out in the historian's own mind before he goes on to confront their results with the historical evidence to be found in his sources. It corresponds to the phase of constructing tentative hypotheses in the work of the natural scientist. By logical relations I mean relations of implication or opposition between categories, or tacit presuppositions, or express beliefs or doctrines. When he has ascertained the currency and influence of a given idea in his period, the historian does well to ask himself, what does this idea logically presuppose, what does it imply, and with what other ideas is it implicitly incompatible—whether or not these logical relations were recognized by those who embraced the idea. For if it should turn out that some of its implications were not recognized, this may become a highly important, though negative, historical fact. Negative facts are of much more significance for the intellectual historian than is usually appreciated. The things that a writer, given his premises, might be expected to say, but doesn't say—the consequences which legitimately and fairly evidently follow from his theses, but which he never sees, or persistently refuses to draw—these may be even more noteworthy than the things he does say or the consequences he does deduce. For they may throw light upon peculiarities of his mind, especially upon his biases and the non-rational elements in his thinking—may disclose to the historian specific points at which intellectual processes have been checked, or diverted, or perverted, by emotive factors. Negative facts of this kind are thus often indicia of positive but unexplicit or subconscious facts. So, again, the determination of not-immediately-obvious *in*compatibilities between ideas may lead to the recognition of the historically instructive fact that one or another writer, or a whole age, has held together, in closed compartments of the mind, contradictory preconceptions or beliefs. Such a fact —like the failure to see necessary positive implications of accepted premises—calls for psychological explanation, if possible; the historian must at least seek for a hypothesis to account for it.

By the psychological relations of ideas, I mean, so to say, elective affinities between them not properly logical in character—the tendency of one, through some process of association by similarity, or often throught the ambiguity of the terms used to express it, to suggest or evoke others. These transitions often pass, with the writers in whom they appear, for logical ones. But especially important for the historian, under this head, is the consideration of the natural *affective* concomitants of various ideas—the kinds of feeling—even, if you like, of "bodily set"—which, when entertained, they tend to arouse, the moods or attitudes to which they are congenial, what I have elsewhere called the "types of metaphysical pathos" which go with various types even of highly abstract notions or doctrines, and are perhaps the real secret of their appeal, at least to the lay public. Philosophy, historically considered, like Nanki Poo in the opera, can sing, and has sung, songs adapted to every—or almost every—changing mood or passion. Into the highly controversial question whether changes of dominant mood beget the philosophies, or changes in philosophy the moods—or sometimes one and sometimes the other—I do not propose here to enter; I merely suggest that the historiographer of ideas must be alert to note the connection between specific ideas and philosophies and specific moods. "Connection" here includes repugnancies. A not uncommon historical phenomenon is a repugnancy between a dominant doctrine in, for example, aesthetics, and the actual tastes of those who feel obliged to subscribe to that doctrine. It has been pointed out by acute students of seventeenth- and eighteenth-century English criticism that most critics of the period seem to have really liked and admired Shakespeare, while the critical principles many of them professed required them to damn him—at least with faint, or much-qualified, praise. This is even more apparent, I think, in those German critics of the early 1790s who were still classicists of the straitest sect, but were, in a few years, to promulgate the new program of *die romantische Poesie*. One factor—though only one—in causing them to reverse their position was, I suspect, that their strong, but repressed, taste for Shakespeare predisposed them to accept a new philosophy of art—and in particular, of poetry—which would justify their taste.

When the intellectual historian of a period has thus considered the logical and the hypothetical psychological relations of the major unit-ideas which he has found prevalent in the period, he must then, of course, return to the historical data, to observe how far the logical relations between these ideas were in fact manifested as operative factors in the thought-tendencies of the time, and what psychological relations among them can be actually seen at work in the minds of their spokesmen. In this latter inquiry he will often, if lucky, be able to discern a sort of genetic relationship between one logically distinct idea and another—to note the nature of the transitions in thought by which one gave rise to a quite different one, and into what combinations or idea-complexes it entered.

For example: the *original* "Romanticists"—the German introducers of the term, the Schlegels and their group [4]—were preoccupied at the outset chiefly with two peculiar problems: (a) What are the essential and distinguishing characteristics of classical, *i.e.*, Greek, art and thought

---

[4] [On this early German Romanticism of the Schlegels and Schiller see especially Lovejoy's two essays, "The Meaning of 'Romantic' in Early German Romanticism" and "Schiller and the Genesis of German Romanticism," in *Essays in the History of Ideas* (Baltimore: Johns Hopkins University Press, 1948), pp. 183–228.]

and culture, on the one hand, and of non-classical, *i.e.*, modern art, etc., on the other? (b) How are these differences to be explained historically? They began their reflection on these problems while still assuming the superiority of the "classical"; their lucubrations on the subject are an episode in the history of the quarrel over the Ancients and Moderns. Now their answer to the second question was that the fundamental differences between classical and "modern" ways of thinking must be due to one or both of the two great historic events which brought the ancient culture to an end: the introduction of Christianity and the invasions of the Nordic or Germanic peoples. This suggested to them, in part, the answer to their other question. If you want to know, in terms of basic ideas—or preconceptions, valuations, or emotional susceptibilities—what distinguishes the classical from the modern or "Romantic," you have but to determine wherein the Christian view of life or of the universe fundamentally differs from the Greek, or the Germanic or Nordic from the Latin or Mediterranean. At first they (certainly Friedrich Schlegel) conceived the former, at least, to be a difference for the worse. But in their attempt—much influenced by Schiller's essay to which I have referred—to formulate the "essence" of the "modern" or Christian *Lebensanschauung,* they came (through processes which, once more, it would take too long to analyze here) to find this in certain propensities or assumptions such as the craving (to which I have already referred) for infinite values or infinite objects for thought or imagination to contemplate, or for the will to aim at, a love of mystery, otherworldliness, an awareness of the duality of man's constitution, a preoccupation with the inner life, and a sense of man's inner corruption—all of these being contrasted with the classical sense for "form" and limits, the supposed Greek love of clarity, absorption in the beauty of this world, "objectivity" (*i.e.*, looking out and not in), untroubled unity of personality, and "serenity." And some, at least, of the former propensities or assumptions these writers found congenial to their own imaginations or temperaments; and they thereupon abruptly turned from what they conceived (with a good deal of historical error) to be the classical mode of art and thought to its opposite, which they had already named "Romantic."

But this conversion was clearly much facilitated by the influence of another idea which has its own pre-history, but was especially potent in the Romantic decades: the idea that a man—and especially an artist—ought to be of his own time, to express in his life or art the characteristics, the ideas, the spirit of his age. He will neither be true to himself, nor *en rapport* with his contemporaries if he does not do so. If, for example, he is a dramatist, he must exhibit in his characters the emotions and motives which he understands—those by which men of his time are moved. A modern man, then, should *be* "modern." But since "modern" or "Romantic" meant mainly, for the early German Romanticists, "Christian," and since for them the spirit of Christianity was best exemplified in the Middle Ages, what at first looked like a sort of revolutionary modernism proved to be identical (in part) with a kind of medievalism.

Now in noting these phenomena which I have roughly sketched, the historian is at once (a) discriminating certain (by no means all) of the more characteristic ideas of the Romantic period, (b) observing the processes by which some of them generated others, and (c) recognizing the complex groupings which they formed in individual—in fact, in numerous individual—minds of the time. When he has done this, the ideas fall into a pattern, of which the diverse modes of relation, logical or psychological, between them are, as it were, the framework. And—though this is perhaps a counsel of perfection—one has not, I think, fully understood the Romantic period as a historic phenomenon—has not grasped what was then going on—until he has apprehended this pattern. It could be at least suggestively portrayed graphically, though the diagram would need to be an extremely large and intricate one.

But when the historian has thus traced these genetic processes, the passing-over from one idea to another, and noted one particular combination of ideas which resulted, he has still to observe that each of the units of *that* complex presently broke loose from its original context and went on its own separate way, generating, in different minds, yet other ideas or entering into other combinations. Thus, out of one group of assumptions made or theorems evolved by the Schlegels, Novalis, and their circle, of which I have tried to suggest roughly the components and their genesis, a whole series of distinct notions and thought-movements emerged. Was it to be assumed, for example, that "modern" or "Romantic" art, as a result of the preoccupation of Christianity with the inner life, is, or should be, peculiarly introspective? Then modern "poetry" has before it as its special province the whole field of subjective states and their infinite nuances, and finds its best expression in the psychological novel or play, especially in those exhibiting subtle moral conflicts in the soul of the hero—already exemplified, or supposed to be exemplified, in Shakespeare's *Hamlet*. This, it will be remembered, is one of the themes of Chateaubriand's *Génie du Christianisme*. With this, the novel, as the form best adapted to this purpose, tended to assume a new dignity and pre-eminence among the literary *genres*. But it was no far cry from this idea to that of the superiority of the *realistic*—but the psychologically realistic—novel in general; so that a French literary historian has not unintelligibly written of "the realism of the Romantics." *Madame Bovary* is certainly neither medieval, nor mysterious, nor vague, nor otherworldly, nor particularly characterized by *Unbegrenztheit*; it has often been described as an attack upon the "Romantic" temper; but it has nevertheless a filiation with one of the elements in the idea-complex of the *Frühromantiker* of the 1790s and the French Romantics of the following decade, as that element developed in isolation from the others. But, on the other hand, Mr. Lascelles Abercrombie assures us that "there is an element directly opposed to romanticism; it is realism." Thus a truly romantic taste in "Views," or landscapes, finds the "pleasant thing in them" to be "a certain blur or dimness, which prevents the eye from being lost in a throng of things positively known, and at the same time stirs one to guess at the infinite possibility the blur contains of things which might be known."

The best thing our minds can do for us is
> In keeping us in hope strange things to see
> That never were, nor are, nor e'er shall be.[5]

Now in insisting that this is the *truly* "romantic" thing, Mr. Abercrombie was simply expressing his own taste in the use of that adjective; but it happens to be true that this note, as well as the other I have just mentioned, was one of the elements in the original idea-complex of the German Romanticists of the 1790s; so that from it a literary tendency opposite to realism could also develop, or at least could gain re-enforcement: the cultivation of a mysterious vagueness, the poetry that hints at what cannot be expressed, at least in words, the art that seeks always to convey a sense of something vast and ineffable in even "the meanest flower that blows." This too is "Romantic" in the sense of one, but only one, of Friedrich Schlegel's definitions: "romantisch—in jenem weitern Sinn des Wortes wo es die Tendenz nach einem tiefen unendlichen Sinn bezeichnet."

In a similar way, then, could be pointed out the later separate fortunes, vicissitudes and alliances of each one of the ideas that constituted the particular combination, in the minds of the original avowed

---

[5] [Lascelles Abercrombie, *Romanticism* (New York: Viking Press, 1927).]

Romanticists, of which I have attempted to indicate summarily the process of formation. But let it not be supposed that this combination contained *all* the new or peculiarly potent ideas of the 1790s. It includes only a group of them which were, at that time, especially associated with the *word* "Romantic." There were others, equally important, which sprang from other sources and developed in other ways—though often absorbed by the same minds and in that sense combined with the former. In the total pattern, these, too, with their relations to the others, would have to be incorporated. But that is too large an enterprise to be attempted here.

II

I suppose, however, that most of the learned company I am addressing are primarily interested in political and social history; but most of the slight illustrations hitherto given of the application of the method of the historian of ideas to the study of the Romantic period have not been obviously pertinent to political or social history. They have had to do with seemingly non-political notions, belonging initially to the fields of literary criticism, aesthetics, or quasi-aesthetic valuations, or religion, or metaphysics. The reason for this lies in a fact which the political historian needs to bear in mind—namely, that most of the new ideas of the 1780s and 1790s *were* originally aesthetic or religious or metaphysical ideas. But they are not on that account less pertinent to political history. For they were the sort of ideas that, when accepted and developed, could modify men's general ways of thinking profoundly, and because profoundly, widely—in many diverse fields, including the political. And if one were to consider the "meaning," in the sense of the historic significance, of—not "Romanticism," but certain ideas of the Romantic period—from the point of view of 1940, their political consequences may well be regarded as the most significant. For a particular group of these ideas, continuously at work on the minds of the educated and reading public for fifteen decades, have produced in our own time a sort of culminating joint-effect, which is at least an essential and conspicuous part of the monstrous scene presented by Germany and by Europe today.[6] That the revolutionary—or counter-revolutionary—political events of the past twenty years would not have

---

[6] [For a critique of Lovejoy's thesis (the connection between Romanticism and Hitlerism) see Leo Spitzer, "Geistesgeschichte vs. History of Ideas as Applied to Hitlerism," *Journal of the History of Ideas*, April 1944, pp. 191–203.]

occurred but for these earlier alterations in fashions of thought, it would be hazardous to maintain. For most of these events are merely new instances of familiar types of historical phenomena which seem to repeat themselves in ages or among peoples whose ruling ideologies are extremely dissimilar. The rise of dictatorships, for example, is an old story. It is, doubtless, possible only under certain conditions; but no uniform underlying general ideas seem to be among those conditions. A political phenomenon which, even in our own time, appears almost simultaneously in, *e.g.*, Germany, Italy, Russia and Spain—countries whose recent intellectual history has certainly been very different— can hardly be explicable as due to the prior prevalence among their peoples of identical fashions of thought. Equally old is the lust of conquest and the emergence of military conquerors on the grand scale— though we had fondly and foolishly supposed the day for such things to be over. I am, therefore, far from suggesting that the rise of the dictatorships and the return of an era of wars of territorial aggrandizement in Europe have their sufficient condition in the changes in ideas which marked the Romantic period; and I recognize that there is room for question whether those changes were even among the necessary conditions for the present recrudescence of those ancient evils. Nevertheless, it is certain—and notorious—that all these contemporary revolutions have had distinctive ideologies—*i.e.*, idea-complexes—associated with them, and that their leaders—some of whom are past masters of practical political psychology—seem to regard the inculcation of these ideologies as indispensable to the success of their revolutionary enterprises and the permanence of the "new orders" they wish to establish. The ideologies may be, in great part they indubitably are, only "rationalizations" of the ambitions, or delusions of grandeur, of the leaders or of the passions of their followers; but even so, the rationalizations are found necessary, before those ambitions are converted into deeds or those latent passions into mass-action. A Hitler or a Mussolini is not more sedulous in the strengthening of his armaments than in the propagating of his ideas—the ideas which, on the one hand, serve his purpose, but on the other, can appeal to the minds of his followers because those minds have already been "conditioned" for their reception.

Now, out of the many "new ideas of the 1780s and 1790s," there were three which—though at the outset they were not political at all in their reference—were destined to be transformed to the domain of political thought and sentiment; to which the German—and in less degree the general European—mind was increasingly conditioned by a series of influential nineteenth-century writers; and the *fusion or combination* of which, I suggest, has been a factor in the production of the state of mind upon which the totalitarian ideologies depend for their appeal. These three are by no means the only ones of which the same might be said; but they are, I incline to think, the most fundamental and most important, though the estimate is certainly debatable. They consist in a sort of apotheosis of conceptions associated with three words; the German words are for the present purpose the most appropriate: *das Ganze, Streben,* and *Eigentümlichkeit.* If terms ending in *-ism* must be had to designate these ideas, they may be called holism or organicism, voluntarism or "dynamism," and diversitarianism.

1. The first—which is now familiar enough—was a relatively new idea about the relation of the individual to the whole—the idea of organism, in its logical or metaphysical sense. The political liberalism of the seventeenth and eighteenth centuries had, it need hardly be recalled, usually conceived the individual as primary. This is the essence of the doctrine of natural rights; it is not really less characteristic of the presuppositions of political utilitarianism. The reality with which politics was concerned was the human person, conceived as a possessor of intrinsic rights, or as a claimant for the means of happiness. He had, admittedly, relations to other individuals, and—at least in the natural rights theory—moral obligations towards them. But the relations and obligations were *between* individuals as such; and though the interests or instincts of the individuals required them to combine in organized aggregates, such as the State, these were secondary, derivative, and merely instrumental to the assurance and adjustment of individual rights or the satisfaction of individual needs and desires. The whole was just the aggregate of its parts, and apart from them was nothing; and the dominant conception of scientific method, like the dominant political theory, proceeded, in its investigation of any complex thing, by an "analysis" or "resolution" of it into its ultimate component parts. To understand *it,* you had but to take it to pieces, to know the parts and *their* characteristics and the laws of their action, and how many of them there were in the given complex—and your problem was solved. But a strain of German thought in the late eighteenth century—which had had earlier fore-shadowings in Shaftesbury, Stahl, and others—tended increasingly towards a reversal of this whole way of thinking—towards giving primacy and a mystical sanctity to what was called "the Idea of the Whole," as defined by Kant in the *Critique of Judgment:* "An Idea [of something] which must determine *a priori* all that is con-

tained in it"—of a "product of nature" in which, "just as every part of it exists *through* all the others, so every part is also thought as existing *for* all the others and for the sake of the Whole (*um . . . des Ganzen willen*), that is, as a tool or organ (*Werkzeug, Organ*)." Kant was talking about a natural organism—a tree; but, as is well known, the conception was speedily carried over into the provinces of metaphysics, of morals and, especially, of politics. The "Idea of the Whole" came increasingly to mean, in its practical application, the idea of the political State. The details of this process are exceedingly various and complex, and cannot be analyzed here; happily, Professor Anderson and Professor Briefs are to deal with some important parts of the story in their papers.[7] But the general result of the repetition of this conception, by many greater and lesser teachers, in diverse forms and with or without qualifications, was the conditioning of the mind of individuals to think of themselves (to a degree perhaps unprecedented in history) as *mere* members of *das Ganze,* as "tools or organs" of the national State—as existing *um des Ganzen willen*—and as finding the interest and value of their existence in the realization of the ends of the State, which are by no means merely the summation of the private ends even of all of its members. Without a long prior conditioning, then, to this idea, among others, the totalitarian ideology would not, I suggest, have the potency that it has, either in Germany or Italy.

The distinguished president of the American Association for the Advancement of Science, Professor Cannon, in his recent presidential address, has argued that the political analogue of the biological organism is democracy, and that "the human body is the best democracy." I venture to disagree, but there is no time to state the distinctions which would justify this disagreement. But in any case the historical effects of a conception, especially of one of the great metaphors which play so large a part in the history of ideas, are not necessarily, or, perhaps, normally identical with its logical implications; and it will, I think, be generally agreed by historians that the vogue of the organismic conception in the nineteenth century has *not* made for what is commonly understood by democracy.

2. But the practical tendency of this idea is profoundly modified by its fusion with another idea of the 1790s. This is the assumption of the primacy, in reality and in value, of process, striving, cumulative

[7] [The reference is to Goetz A. Briefs, "The Economic Philosophy of Romanticism," and Eugene N. Anderson, "German Romanticism as an Ideology of Cultural Crisis," *Journal of the History of Ideas,* June 1941, pp. 279–317.]

becoming, over any static consummation—the dislike of finality, *das Abgeschlossene*, and in particular, the peculiar sensibility to the pathos of struggle, which is, by necessary implication, a struggle *against* something or somebody, some *Anstoss* or antagonist. *Streben*, as everyone knows, was one of the most sacred words of the German Romantics—and it was necessarily, for them, a *Streben ins Unendliche*, a striving without a terminus; and in spite of the various other senses and applications which this formula could and did receive, its vogue tended in the main towards that apotheosis of "the Will" which, astonishingly combined in Schopenhauer with its polar opposite, a Vedantist and Buddhistic quietism and otherworldliness, found its natural culmination in Nietzsche's gospel of the *Wille zur Macht*, that "Dionysian philosophy" of which "the decisive feature," as he writes in *Ecce Homo*, is "the yea-saying to contradiction and war, the postulation of Becoming, together with the radical rejection even of the concept *Being*"—the "tragic" temper which seeks "to be far beyond terror and pity and to be the eternal lust of Becoming itself—that lust which also involves the joy of destruction." The notion of *Streben* was originally, and even in Nietzsche largely remained, an ideal for the individual. But it too, naturally enough, has been converted into a political idea; and Nietzsche, as Professor Brinton has shown, has become the chief official philosopher of Nazism—after Hitler. But as a political idea, this second notion has been fused with the first. The individual, as essentially an organ of *das Ganze*, the state, does his striving through the state, which is the embodiment of the Will to Power. If it is to be effective in this capacity, it must be completely integrated; it can permit no struggles within itself, between its parts—for example, no class-struggle and no party-conflicts. The parts must be strictly regimented, *gleichgeschaltet*, for the service of the whole. But the nation or State itself takes on the role of the insatiable Romantic hero—in which its members can, indeed, vicariously share. It must ever strive for expansion, external power, and yet more power, not as a regrettably necessary means to some final rationally satisfying goal, but because continuous self-assertion, transcending of boundaries, triumph over opposition, is its vocation. As the personification of the present German State, Adolf Hitler is Carlyle's "infinite bootblack" endowed with all the power of a great people and a vast military machine. It is true that, somewhere in *Mein Kampf*, Hitler shows, in one passage, some embarrassment at the thought of the finitude of this planet. When the "superior man," *der höchsstehende Mensch*, through struggle has once made himself master of the world, there will be no more opportunity for struggle, but only a tedious reign of universal peace. But Hitler puts the awkward thought from his mind; the evil day is at least a long way off; *also erst Kampf, und dann kann man sehen was zu machen ist.* Hitler is, in short, a kind of vulgar, political and sanguinary Faust, *der immer strebend sich bemüht* upon the international scene—a Faust, I need hardly add, before his redemption.

3. One of the most revolutionary of the ideas of the 1790s was an assertion of the value of diversity in human opinions, characters, tastes, arts and cultures. This had, it is true, a long pre-history, which cannot be told here, but in the original German Romanticists of that decade it reached a climax and become one of the chief articles of their creed. It was revolutionary because it reversed a presupposition that had been dominant for some two centuries: the presupposition which may be called uniformitarianism. By this term I do not mean the assumption that individuals and peoples are *in fact* identical in their characters and beliefs and ways of living. It was evident—to the reformer of the Enlightenment all too painfully evident—that they are not. Uniformitarianism is the assumption that what is most important, most valuable, normal, in men consists in what is the same in all men, and that their actual diversities in opinion and cultures and forms of government are evidences of departures from the norm of human life. And this was a natural and seemed an obvious inference from a very common assumption concerning the nature of truth. To any given question that can be asked or any practical problem with which men are confronted, it seemed evident that there can be only one true or correct answer. There is one right generic way of performing any kind of task—of writing a play or an epic, painting a landscape, building a house, organizing and governing a society—and (this was a postulate usually tacitly or explicitly associated with the uniformitarian preconception) any man having normal human faculties is capable of discovering the one true view or the one correct rule of practice, for himself, by the unaided—provided it be also the uncorrupted—light of nature. For there is, in that admittedly very mixed compound called human nature, a faculty, the *gemeine Menschenverstand,* which is the organ for apprehending or revealing the one true answer to any question to which an answer is needful for man, the universal and invariant objective truth. What is rational is uniform; and what is not uniform is *eo ipso* not rational; and diversity is therefore the easily recognizable mark of error. In a sense, every man has a latent potential knowledge of such truth, by virtue of

his possession of *le bon sens ou raison* which, as Descartes declared, is *la chose du monde la mieux partagée* and is *naturellement égale en tous les hommes*—and therefore has nothing to do with time or place or race. But in most of mankind it has been buried under a vast mass of accumulated error—that is to say, of differences in beliefs, valuations, laws, practices. These errors were the product of a long, increasing series of unhappy accidents—*i.e.*, of lapses from rationality on the part of the multitude, misled by a few men actuated by the love of power—priests and kings. The vehicles of the transmission of these errors—what were called *les préjugés*—from generation to generation, were tradition, custom (whose tyranny was so bitterly denounced by Montaigne and Charron and many lesser writers), and above all, the early education of children. The task of the lover of humanity, the reformer, the educator, therefore, was less to discover and show to men new truths, than to purge their minds of the historic accretion of non-rational prejudices, and thus to allow the pure, clear light of nature within them to shine forth of itself. For, among all the extremely numerous senses of the sacred word "nature," in its normative use, from the sixteenth to the late eighteenth century, the most common and potent was that in which it summed up this whole uniformitarian complex of ideas.

But to the Romantics of the 1790s (following Herder) it appeared that the diversity of men and ages and peoples, in their ways of thinking and feeling and expressing themselves in arts and institutions, is "natural" and necessary, and also supremely desirable and right. And from this pregnant premise they drew two opposite consequences, of which the second was to prevail over the first. The assumption made initially for tolerance and catholicity. All the historic manifestations of human nature are good, and the cultivated man will train himself to appreciate and enjoy them all. But the other inference was that it is the first duty of an individual or a people to cherish and intensify the differentness, idiosyncrasy, *Eigentümlichkeit*, with which nature has endowed him or it. This, like the ideal of *Streben*, was, at the outset, applied largely to the individual, especially to the artist; but it also tended to be applied, and in the end to be chiefly applied, to the nation or race. So applied, it eventually destroyed, in many minds, the conception of a universal standard of human conduct and the sense of a common human destiny. It gave respectability to what the eighteenth century had meant by *les préjugés*.. It seemed to lend a new philosophic sanction to that unreflective or animal nationalism which had long been a potent factor in European politics, but which, in the *Aufklärung*, had appeared to be on the wane among enlightened men. It tended to substitute for the piety towards humanity as such an exclusive piety towards one's own folk and its peculiarities; the very word "humanity," beloved by the earlier liberals, began to be *démodé,* and it became, as is well known, almost a commonplace in the Romantic period to say that there are no "men" but only Frenchmen, Germans, Englishmen, *et al.* Finally, when combined with that "permanent affective element of human nature," the collective, mutually re-enforcing *amour-propre* of the group, it was easily transformed into a conviction of the superiority of what is distinctive of one's own people—its "blood," its *Volksgeist,* traditions, *mores* and institutions—and of its right to dominate all lesser breeds.

Of these three among the ideas of the 1790s, any one, by itself, might have worked out to historic issues quite different from those that actually resulted—and, in fact, when not combined with the others, did so. For example, if the first had not been combined with the third, the "whole" to which the individual is to subordinate himself and whose ends he is to seek might have been construed as humanity—which is, in fact, the only real social totality—and a tendency towards this interpretation may be seen in Novalis's *Die Christenheit oder Europa;* and the second and third, when taken as ideals for the individual, have always been at variance with the first. But when, and in so far as, these three ideas are (however incongruously) combined, one may discern, I think, an important part (though, assuredly, far from all) of the pattern of ideas behind—or associated with—the fateful political events of our own time: the idea of a national State whose members are but instruments to its own vaster ends; in which, therefore, no internal oppositions or disagreements in individual opinion can be permitted; which, however, is itself dedicated to a perpetual struggle for power and self-enlargement, with no fixed goal or terminus, and is animated by an intense and obsessing sense of the differentness of its own folk, of their duty of *keeping* different and uncorrupted by any alien elements, and by a conviction of the immeasurable value of their supposedly unique characteristics and culture. A host of other factors and events between the 1790s and the present, of which nothing has been said here, have, of course, contributed to this outcome; I have merely attempted to suggest, in a deplorably but unavoidably sketchy fashion, that there is a certain specific historical connection between the intellectual revolution of the Romantic period and the tragic spectacle of Europe in 1940.

THE MARXIST OUTLOOK *

H. B. Acton †

By a "world-outlook" I mean a systematic account of the nature of
the world which claims, by showing the place of man in the scheme
of things, to indicate the point and purpose of his life. The theory of
the world is often called a metaphysical theory and the theory of conduct
an ethical or moral theory. In my opinion the clarification and criticism
of world-outlooks is a fundamental part of philosophy. Indeed, I hardly
think that philosophy would have existed as something distinct from
science or poetry but for the tendency to attempt some explanation of
the world as the scene of human endeavour. When Kant referred to
"the inevitable problems of pure reason" about "God, freedom, and
immortality," he was referring in a summary way to the fundamental
philosophical task of analysing and criticizing world-outlooks, a task
that may be undertaken even by those philosophers who do not believe
that any world-outlook is or could be adequate. It is clear, of course,
that the civilized religions, since they seek to show how human conduct
fits in with some Divine Plan or Cosmic Conflict, have world-outlooks.
It is, however, misleading to look upon religions and world-outlooks
as the same thing, as some people do. For in ordinary usage religion
involves belief in supernatural beings and conduct regulated in the
light of this belief, but according to some world-outlooks (e.g. that of
Spinoza) there are no supernatural beings, while according to others
(e.g. Epicureanism) beings may exist deserving that description but
human conduct need take no account of them.

Marxism is such a non-religious world-outlook. Its theory of the
world is known as Dialectical Materialism and its theory of human
purpose as Scientific Socialism.[1] . . .

---

* Reprinted from *Philosophy* (The Journal of the Royal Institute of Philosophy), Nov. 1947, pp. 208–211, 213–229. Copyright 1947 by *Philosophy*. Used
by permission of *Philosophy* and the author.

† Harry B. Acton is Professor of Philosophy at the University of London. He
is also Director of the Royal Institute of Philosophy and editor of its journal
Philosophy.

[1] [For the philosophical background of Marxism the reader is referred especially to Sidney Hook, *From Hegel to Marx* (New York: Reynal & Hitchcock,
1936); and Herbert Marcuse, *Reason and Revolution. Hegel and the Rise of*

Dialectical Materialism

It is well known that Marxists claim to be materialists and in what follows I shall first attempt to show what they mean by so describing themselves. It should be noticed at the outset, however, that the word materialism is frequently used in a moral sense to stigmatize those persons who selfishly aim at material goods and luxuries. I need hardly say that it is not in this sense that Marxists regard themselves as materialists although, as we shall see later, they do apply their materialist theory to the moral sphere.

The first thing that Marxists mean when they call themselves materialists is that they believe the material world exists independently of anyone's perception of it. That is, they hold the view of perception which philosophers to-day call Realism. . . .

The most sustained discussion of these matters from a Marxist standpoint that I know of is in Lenin's *Materialism and Empirio-Criticism* which he completed in London in 1908 and published in Moscow in 1909. By "Empirio-Criticism" Lenin means the phenomenalist theories of perception and knowledge developed by Ernst Mach and Richard Avenarius and kindred thinkers.[2] Some of Lenin's fellow members of the Social Democratic Party had been attracted by these views which they thought consistent with the Marxist philosophy. Lenin thought they were not and wrote his book to demonstrate this.

What positive arguments then does he put forward in favour of a realist theory of perception? His most important argument, I think, is that no amount of philosophical argument can weigh against the philosopher's own practice when he eats his meals and talks to his friends. The phenomenalist or idealist conducts himself in much the same way as the naïve realist does and therefore, according to Lenin, his deeds belie what his arguments claim to show. Lenin says that Diderot came close to the view of contemporary materialism "that arguments

Social Theory (New York: The Humanities Press, 1954). On Marxism in general and in relation to other intellectual movements see also G. D. H. Cole, *A History of Socialist Thought* (New York: St. Martin's Press, 1953–1960); Sir Isaiah Berlin, *Karl Marx. His Life and Environment* (London, New York: Oxford University Press, 1952); Jacques Barzun, *Darwin, Marx, Wagner* (Boston: Little, Brown and Company, 1941); Edmund Wilson, *To the Finland Station* (Garden City: Doubleday & Company, 1940).]

[2] [Phenomenalism, in contrast to Lenin's materialism, jettisoned all metaphysics. Experience alone is real; metaphysical ultimates, whether God and the soul or matter and atoms, are only "mental artifices."]

and syllogisms alone would not suffice to refute materialism, and that it is not a question of theoretical argument," and after quoting with approval Plekhanov's remark that belief in the existence of the external world is an inevitable *salto vitale* (vital leap) in philosophy, he writes: "From the standpoint of life, practice ought to be the first and fundamental criterion of the theory of knowledge. It inevitably leads to materialism, brushing aside the infinite inventions of professorial scholasticism." It may be remembered that Descartes, in endeavouring to prove the existence of the material world from his own existence and experiences laid some weight upon the "teachings of nature," and that since his day various philosophers have regarded the independent existence of a material world and of other selves as unassailable Principles of Common Sense. Lenin, I am sure, would not have quarrelled with this language, but I think he would have insisted that it is not merely a question of listening to nature's promptings but also of acting on them. We have an irresistible tendency to believe in the existence of a material world but it is because we have come successfully to act on it that we are justified in taking it as the basis of our theorising. Thus, in perception we leap in thought from our sensations to a material world that causes them and when we come to act we constantly find material things and people who respond. We therefore divide our theory from our practice if we adopt an idealist or phenomenalist theory of perception, and this is either foolish or dishonest. . . .

Lenin also argues against phenomenalism that it is inconsistent with the scientifically established view that the physical world existed before there were conscious beings to have sensations of it. If the material world consists of sensations and sensations depend on living organisms then the material world could not have existed before there were living organisms, and the scientific account of the development of the world is a dream. . . .

It seems to me, therefore, that Lenin was right in rejecting phenomenalism. What form of realism, however, does he in consequence accept? I am afraid that we cannot find in his or in the writings of Marx and Engels anything approaching a satisfactory realist account of perception. Engels writes (*Ludwig Feuerbach*): "The influences of the external world upon man express themselves in his brain, are reflected therein as feelings, thoughts, instincts, volitions . . ." According to Lenin our perceptions are "images of the outer world," and he writes of "a reality which is copied, photographed, and reflected by our sensations . . ."

The second thing that Marxists mean when they call themselves materialists is that the existence of matter preceded that of mind and that mind arose out of matter. Engels describes this in his *Ludwig Feuerbach* as the theory of "nature as primary." In *Materialism and Empirio-Criticism,* Lenin puts the view in the following way: "Materialism, in full agreement with natural science, takes matter as the *prius,* regarding consciousness, reason, and sensation as derivative, because in a well expressed form it is connected only with the higher forms of matter (organic matter)." Those who hold that mind is prior to matter assume according to Engels, "world creation in some form or other," and therefore those who maintain the primacy of matter deny the existence of a Creator. Thus Marxist materialism is atheistic.

Marxist philosophers, however, do not embark on detailed criticism of theistic arguments. Engels, in *Ludwig Feuerbach,* gives a brief account of the development of the notion of "the one exclusive god of the monotheistic religions" from the dream apparitions of primitive man, much as Tylor and Spencer had done. In this way atheism is established by showing how the notion of God can be explained in natural terms as a projection of human desires and illusions.[3] If we object that even if the notion has arisen in that way it does not follow that there is no divine reality corresponding to it, the Marxist will stress the phrase of Lenin's quoted above that materialism is "in full agreement with natural science." Marxists, I think, are positivists to the extent that they consider the only reliable knowledge of the world is that obtained by the methods of the sciences, although, as I have shown, they reject the phenomenalism that generally goes with this view. In the *German Ideology,* for instance, Marx and Engels write: "When reality is depicted, philosophy as an independent branch of activity loses its medium of existence." Here, it is true, Marx and Engels are particularly concerned with human society. But in his *Anti-Dühring* Engels writes: "That which still survives of all earlier philosophy is the science of thought and its laws—formal logic and dialectics. Everything else is subsumed in the positive science of Nature and history." There is no God because the sciences do not reveal one. . . .

The third main element in Marxist materialism (the first two are epistemological realism and the view that matter existed before mind

[3] [Marx and Engels took over this idea from Ludwig Feuerbach (1804–1872) whose *Essence of Christianity,* translated into English by George Eliot, created a sensation when it first appeared in 1841.]

in the absence of a Creator) is its claim to be dialectical. To explain in full what this means would involve an excursion into the history of philosophy for which there is no space here and so I confine my account to the barest minimum.

Dialectical materialism is contrasted by Marxists with the mechanical materialism of the eighteenth century. According to Engels, eighteenth century science still worked largely with notions built up in the science of mechanics and failed to take account of what is peculiar to the chemical and biological sciences but rather tried to "reduce" these to mechanics. If I understand the position correctly, dialectical materialism does not merely admit but emphasizes that in the passage of time novel types of entity have come into being based upon those that already existed, but with features not reducible to those of their generators. This view is closely akin to the theory of Emergent Evolution advocated by Lloyd Morgan (a writer known to and quoted by Lenin) and Samuel Alexander.[4] That this is the Marxist view is, I think, shown by some curious remarks about matter and consciousness made by Lenin in *Materialism and Empirio-Criticism*. Lenin was quite sure that without brains there would be no thinking and even accepted the expression that thinking was a "function of the brain." But he objected to a statement by Dietzgen that "the intangible idea is also material and real" with the remark: "But to call thought material is to make an erroneous step, is to confuse materialism and idealism." It seems likely that by this and a similar statement, Lenin means that consciousness, while based on the existence of brains, is not reducible to a series of physical and chemical changes, but has some unique characteristics not to be found elsewhere. If I am right, Lenin is criticizing the theory named by Professor Broad Reductive Materialism in favour of the theory he calls Emergent Materialism, according to which, "mentality is an emergent characteristic."

From what has already been said it will be seen that dialectical materialism is an evolutionary theory according to which from time to time in the processes of change, a gradual accumulation of differences is suddenly succeeded by the emergence of something quite new. I have illustrated this by reference to the emergence of life and consciousness, a topic which naturally interests everyone. The Marxists held, however,

[4] Referred to by Professor Haldane (*The Marxist Philosophy and the Sciences*, p. 150), as "the only academic philosopher in England whose system has any serious affinity with Marxism".

that sudden transformations of gradually accumulated changes into a new character may be observed in detail in the various parts of nature. According to Mr. Shirokov's *Textbook of Marxist Philosophy*: [5]

Quantitative changes at a determined stage lead inevitably to changes of quality. Solid iron may be heated in greater or less degree and still remain a piece of iron. However, when the heat reaches a certain point it causes the iron to melt and enter into a qualitatively different state. Capitalist enterprises though they may be on a big or little scale yet have their higher and lower limits of magnitude. Complete capitalist planning as between all industries is too big a task for capitalism. From the other aspect a capitalist undertaking can by no means be as small as it likes.

Scientists who profess the Marxist philosophy have collected many examples of this process of the transformation of quantity into quality, as they call it, but I do not think that they would have thought it worth while to do this unless they were seeking for some cosmic justification of their belief that to look forward to a sudden transformation of human society was "scientific." The juxtaposition of solid iron with capitalist planning in the passage quoted above suggests this.

Marxists regard it as a merit of their view of evolution that it does not merely emphasize, as non-Marxists do not, the sudden emergence of novelty, but also explains how it is that development takes place at all. According to Marxists the motive force of all change and development is an internal contradiction in what changes. Lenin in his *Philosophical Notebooks* writes: "In its proper meaning, dialectics is the study of the contradiction *within the very essence of things.*" He also refers to *"the mutually exclusive* and opposed tendencies in all the phenomena and processes of nature (including spirit and society)" as "the identity" or "unity" of opposites. The identity or unity of opposites, he holds, is only transitory, "the struggle of the mutually exclusive opposites is absolute, as movement and evolution are." Engels gives the simple case of movement of a particle as an illustration. "Motion itself is a contradiction: even simple mechanical change of place can only come about through a body at the same moment of time being both in one place and another place, being in one and the same place and also not in it." Other examples given by Engels and Lenin are: the plus and minus signs in mathematics, positive and negative electricity in physics, the

[5] Translated by A. A. Moseley, revised and edited by John Lewis, Gollancz. The last three parts of this book were prepared under the auspices of the Leningrad Institute of Philosophy.

class struggle in the social sciences. All change, then, occurs through contradiction or opposition. Evolutionary change, according to the Marxists, takes place through a process they call "the negation of the negation." Process A is opposed by its contradictory not-A, and, let us suppose, A is *succeeded* by not-A. Not-A, in its turn, however, will be the pole of a further opposition and so will be succeeded by its opposite, A. This second A, however, will not be merely the first A reinstated, for the first A was the opposite of a not-A that had not yet replaced it, while the second A is the opposite of a not-A which has already replaced the original A. The outline of this conception was clearly put by the late David Guest when he wrote: "that development takes place in a kind of spiral, one change negating a given state of affairs and a succeeding change, which negated the first, re-establishing (in a more developed form, or "on a higher plane" as it is often expressed) some essential feature of the original state of affairs." Engels gives the example of a grain of barley planted in the ground. This is "negated" by the plant that succeeds it. This in its turn, however, is negated (the negation of the negation) by its own decay. "As a result of this negation of the negation we have once again the original grain of barley, but not as a single unit, but ten, twenty or thirty fold."

We learn from Engels's *Anti-Dühring* that Dühring criticized Marx's use of the principle of the negation of the negation on the ground that it is used as "the midwife to deliver the future from the womb of the past," and, indeed, objected to the whole Marxist theory of contradiction in the nature of things on the ground that contradiction, negation, etc., are logical terms with no application at all to the material world. As a teacher of Philosophy, and so, according to Lenin, a "scientific salesman of theology," I feel some sympathy with Dühring on this issue. As to the negation of the negation, Engels's answer in effect was that Marx did not use that principle as a premise from which to conclude that socialism must come out of capitalism, but found, from an empirical examination of social trend and structure, that that was the pattern they in fact displayed. And as to the contradictions and oppositions, Engels was quite sure they existed in nature as a whole as well as in human society. He assures his readers, however, that the three principles of dialectic (the union of opposites, the transformation of quantity into quality, the negation of the negation) are only very general laws which find embodiment in very different ways in the different spheres to which they apply. If, then, these principles cannot be used as premises of scientific arguments, and if the particular laws of natural development have to be discovered by the ordinary empirical methods known to non-Marxist scientists, their positive use in science must be slight. Outside the social sciences, Marxist scientists seem to proceed much as non-Marxists, except that the former, unlike the latter, find it a cause for satisfaction when they can show that the results of scientific research can be fitted into the dialectical scheme. Since, however, the dialectical terms such as "contradiction," "opposition," and "negation" are used in an extremely vague and elastic manner, there is naturally little difficulty in securing a fit. As I have already suggested, Marxists are primarily interested in social themes and seek for the dialectic in inanimate nature mainly in order to sustain and enhance their faith in the dialectical march of history. . . .

Scientific Socialism

According to Lenin, it was Marx and Engels who showed "how to carry materialism into the domain of the social sciences." One thing that this means is that Lenin regarded Marx and Engels as the first to apply scientific methods to the social sciences. Whether he was right in so regarding them we need not discuss, but we must examine a further introductory statement he makes on the application of materialism to the social sphere. "Consciousness in general," he says, "reflects being—this is the general position of *all* materialism. It is impossible not to see its direct and *inseparable* connection with the position of historical materialism, that is, that social consciousness *reflects* social being." Lenin reinforces this with a further argument. "Materialism generally recognizes the objectively real being (matter) as existing independently of mind, sensation, experience, etc. Historical materialism recognizes social being as existing independently of the social consciousness of humanity. Consciousness here and there is only an image of being, at best an approximately true (adequate, ideally exact) image of it.". . .

However, while Marxists do use the fallacious argument that materialism in the realm of non-human nature involves social materialism, that is by no means their main argument for historical materialism. Historical materialism is advanced by means of much more direct arguments. The most successful of these, it seems to me, is that sketched out by Marx in his *Theses on Feuerbach*. Prior to his own day, Marx held, materialist thinkers saw how man was subject to natural and social influences upon which his happiness or misery depended, and they put forward plans showing how to ameliorate the conditions of man by changing those influences which caused his misery. Thus Robert Owen [6] showed how faulty social and industrial arrangements caused unhappiness and crime and indicated, both in argument and by example, the sort of changes that would educate men to virtue and happiness. But this, Marx suggests in the third of his *Theses on Feuerbach,* is to ignore two fundamental points. In the first place this sort of procedure really assumes that there are two parts of society, one part consisting of those who might reform society, the other part consisting of the society to be reformed. More than this, the assumption is that there are reformers outside the society who, like gods, can put it right. But reformers are necessarily in society, and so, in the second place, it is necessary to ask how it can happen that anyone should want and try to reform his society. The pre-Marxist materialist reformers forgot that "circumstances are changed by men and that the educator himself must be educated." This line of argument was pursued further by Engels in his *Anti-Dühring* where he argued that the Utopian socialists had omitted to consider why it was that their admirable schemes for social improvement which commended themselves to the "reason" of enlightened eighteenth and nineteenth century thinkers, were prepared at that time and, "reasonable" as they were, provoked laughter and opposition from those who might have implemented them. There surely must be some forces in society which both led to an outburst of Utopian theories and also prevented them from being put into practice on any decisive scale.

In my opinion these arguments are sound. Marx and Engels have formulated the very important social truths (a) that all members of a society are subject to its social forces, (b) that not all social changes that appear desirable are, in that society, practicable, and (c) that only those social changes are practicable which can be linked with a sufficiently powerful existing social agency. These are truths which men of affairs have acted on for centuries, but this does not detract from the scientific importance of formulating them. The contribution of Marx and Engels to our understanding of this aspect of society is most valuable, particularly if we compare it with the roughly contemporary statements of Comte [7] that the evils against which he, like Marx and Engels, protested, could be removed by setting up a "Spiritual Power" that would unite society. However, these truths alone do not constitute

---

[6] [The English "Utopian Socialist" (1771–1858).]
[7] [The French Positivist (1798–1852).]

historical materialism. For to (a) must be added the vital corollary that the fundamental social force which determines all the rest is the method of production operating in the society, and further propositions have to be added to the effect that social evolution advances through class struggles and that within our own society the force to which schemes for its beneficent transformation must, if they are to succeed, be linked, is the proletariat. When these truths are understood, says Mr. Stalin, "Socialism is converted from a dream of a better future for humanity into a science."

Clearly, I cannot pretend even to touch on the theme of Scientific Socialism without saying something about the way in which the means and conditions of material production are supposed to determine both the forms of society and the spiritual productions of mankind. The crucial passages from the *Critique of Political Economy* and the *Anti-Dühring* have been so often quoted that it would be idle for me to reproduce them yet again. For a very clear and brief statement I would refer those interested to Marx's letter to P. V. Annenkov of December 28, 1846, and to the *German Ideology*. In the first, Marx says that society is "the product of man's reciprocal activity," and goes on to argue that men cannot behave towards one another as they choose, since they are born into a society with its ways already established. What has determined the ways we find are "the productive forces won by the previous generation." In the *German Ideology*, Marx and Engels have more to say about the "productive forces." What distinguishes men from animals is that they "*produce* their means of subsistence." In order to produce their means of subsistence they must use their hands and, later, such tools as they can devise. In working with their hands and tools they necessarily come into contact with one another in ways which the work they are doing and the tools they are handling will determine. Their life and their acts are the same thing, and as they work with others, so their life will be. Important among the means of production will be, of course, their language, without which complicated social tasks would be impossible. The discovery of a new way of producing their means of subsistence (e.g. the taming of wild animals) will change their mode of working and so the way in which the individuals fit together will be a different one, and the structure of the society will have altered. They will then have a different mode of life, act differently, talk differently, be different men. "Men are the producers of their conceptions, ideas, etc.—real, active men, as they are conditioned by a definite development of their productive forces and of the intercourse corresponding to these, up to its furthest forms. Consciousness can never be anything else than conscious existence, and the existence of men is their actual life process."

When a theory seems obviously true to some intelligent people and obviously false to others, it is probable that the contending parties have a different understanding of the point at issue. Now I think there is some misunderstanding about the point at issue in the materialist conception of history. If a people change their way of getting their living then consesquential changes are inevitable, for the very simple reason that they will find themselves in different situations which will call for different conduct. When, for instance, a pastoral people commence agriculture, sooner or later arrangements will have to be made for keeping people from trampling the growing crops and so a control over land will develop different from anything that had obtained before. At the risk of some measure of sophistication we may say that agricultural society requires a different law and morality from those which exist in pastoral society. It is not possible to start agricultural production without at the same time organizing access to the land and its protection from those who might damage it. The hunters and the farmers must arrange their conduct towards one another. Thus, to say that a change in methods of production will cause a change in law and morality is uncommonly like a tautology. It is not so much that the one change brings about the other as that the change is all really one change. It is also part of the same change that farmers will think differently from hunters. They will think more of seeds and harvests and less of spoors and camping grounds. All this, I suggest, is undeniable, and it is this that is rightly asserted by the upholders of the materialist conception of history.

Then what is being denied by those who deny the theory? What opponents of the theory are denying, I think, is the proposition that the only way in which a society's law, morality, and thought is changed is by changes in its means of production. It is possible, they argue, for the law of a society to be made more subtle, for its morality to be made more rational, for its thinking to become more effective, even though no new tools are discovered or no new means devised of using the old ones. They argue further that some thinker (say an Egyptian mathematician) might invent a device (say a means of measurement) which will be used to improve the methods of production (say the remarking of constantly flooded land), and so demonstrate the power of thought over production. Marxists, when faced with this type of argument do not contest it. Rather do they say that to deny it would be undialectical. The means of production form the basis of society but the superstructure of thought and morality are not inert, but in their turn interact with the basis from which they spring. Once we get to disputing which of various social "factors" is "predominant" there will be no end to argument as Plekhanov pointed out in his *Materialist Conception of History*. Marxists tend to argue, however, that it is the spur of need and the urge to help on our productive resources that lead men to elaborate their law or develop their science. In this, however, I think they exaggerate. Genuine products of the nineteenth century as they were, Marx and Engels were quite convinced that life is work. So, of course, it was and is for many. But there are few for whom life is nothing but work, and at both ends of the social scale there are people for whom it contains little work at all. On what grounds is it then maintained that it is the working period that necessarily determines the whole nature of the life? The ground that may be offered is that without work (production) life cannot be maintained. But it by no means follows from this that the working period is the sole determinant of man's nature. I think it is this mistaken view that leads to the widely held Marxist theory that science is the child of industry. It is undeniable that craft and industry have been important factors in the development of the natural sciences. But what Veblen calls "idle curiosity," an activity of leisure rather than of industry and pursued for its own sake alone, is equally necessary for the growth of science as we know it.

There is a further element in the view sketched out in the *German Ideology* which, it seems to me, is often lost sight of. This is the pronouncement made in the sentence I have already quoted: "Consciousness can never be anything else than conscious existence, and the existence of men is their actual life process." In this passage, I think, Marx is stressing not so much the materialism of his view as its concreteness. His point, as I see it, is that the man who thinks is the same man as the man who works, loves, and eats, so that to consider his thoughts apart from his other activities is to consider them in the abstract and not as they really are. Furthermore, according to Marx to consider human nature apart from the real activities of men at a given time and place is also to make a misleading abstraction. Just as there is no thought that is not part of some man's life process, so there is no human nature that is not the nature of given men living in definite ways.[8] This part of the *German Ideology* is advocating an empirical approach to the study of human society untrammelled by preconception about what is and what is not "natural" to mankind. The contention, I suggest, is sound irrespective of Marx's views on the supreme influence of work. . . .

The primary aim of socialists has been to set up a form of society free from the economic injustices of the prevailing social order. Their opponents have generally replied that, while the injustices may be mitigated, they cannot be removed because they are rooted in fundamental elements of human nature. Socialists frequently counter by maintaining that human nature is different from what the defenders of the present order say it is and that men will work for the public good as well as for private gain. Marxist socialists, however, do not take part in this sort of argument at all. In their view capitalist society is by its own operations producing within itself a new society which will ultimately remove the economic injustices by transforming the order that creates them. The moving force arises in the industrial system itself which requires for its working a proletariat who are at present exploited but who will inevitably decide to control the system themselves. It follows therefore that the way to obtain a socialist order is to work with the proletariat to that end. They are the existing social force destined to establish a socialist society.

I should like to make the following comments on the view thus inadequately sketched.

1. It assumes that there are social trends which proceed even though no one deliberately aims at producing them. In this, I think, Marxists are correct, since there is no reason to suppose that the result of many different and conflicting aims will be the achievement of any single one of them. Marxists also think, however, that they know in general what the course of social development will be. Such confidence, I should have thought, is not justified. How can we assess its value? In the same way, I suggest, as we assess the confidence of any putative scientist—by seeing whether his predictions and experiments come off. . . .

2. Let us suppose, for the sake of argument, that the Marxists are

[8] [There has been considerable debate recently about Marx's conception of "human nature." On this point see Erich Fromm, *Marx's Concept of Man* (New York: Frederick Ungar Publishing Company, 1961); and a fine article by Daniel Bell, "The Debate on Alienation," in Leopold Labedz (ed), *Revisionism. Essays on the History of Marxist Ideas* (New York: Frederick A. Praeger, Inc., 1962).]

right in believing that they have a scientific understanding of the processes of history and can descry its main future trend. How, then, can this knowledge affect human conduct and morality? According to Marx and Engels, "freedom is knowledge of necessity." Before we know the laws of physical nature we do not control nature but are controlled by it. When we understand natural laws we can foresee some of the future and act on the world in ways which serve our purposes. Similarly, so long as we are ignorant of the laws of social development social events appear to us as arbitrary and unforeseeable, but once we have a scientific knowledge of social forces, once we "grasp their action, their direction, and their effects," we can "subject them more and more to our will." This parallel between the knowledge that gives us control over the physical world and the knowledge that gives us control over society is plausible, but I suggest, misleading. For the "we" who, through knowledge of natural laws control nature and are to that extent free, are mankind as a whole, a set of beings distinct by their possession of reason, from the world they are controlling. But who are the "we" who by their knowledge of social laws, are to control society? Marx himself has taught us not to regard ourselves as outside society. It is therefore important that we should be clear about who does the controlling, and who is controlled when we have a social science to guide our actions. Auguste Comte thought that the social scientists should control the rest. The Marxists clearly wish to say that society will understand and so regulate itself. In fact, however, there will be some people who claim to know the direction society is taking and will like it, and there will be others who won't think society is going that way and in any case won't think it a desirable way. The result as Marxists anticipate, is struggle, and if they have predicted well, the control will be by the proletarian victors until all have come to see the necessity of the process. The difference between Marx and Comte is not so great after all. Both are exponents of government by social scientists and both, I think, tended to think that the way to choose a social ideal is to find what the society is moving to and want that. We are asked in effect to bow down before the future conqueror whose advent we may delay but cannot prevent.

3. It is characteristic of Utopian thinking to criticize the present in terms of an ideal future but to give only perfunctory attention to the means of passing from the present bad to the hoped-for better condition. Undoubtedly the Marxists have improved on the Utopians in this respect by showing that reforms can only be carried out by men who

know how to make use of the possibilities inherent in their society. It seems to me, however, that the leading Marxist thinkers have given far too little thought to the moral problems involved in movements towards a classless society. Engels says that each class has its own morality and Mr. T. A. Jackson, expanding this point, writes: "In a class-divided society there are and must be *as many positive moralities as there are classes.* That is why class struggles in their full development permit of no compromise: that is why they must be fought out to a finish." In consequence the existence of any morality that transcends classes tends to be questioned or at least its efficacy is denied. And both Engels and Marx stigmatized as "petit-bourgeois" Proudhon's attempt to show how moral principles ought to apply in the economic sphere. . . .

SOME ASPECTS OF DARWIN'S INFLUENCE UPON MODERN THOUGHT *

Arthur O. Lovejoy

The subject assigned me by the Secretary of the Academy of Science is "Darwin's Influence upon Modern Thought." [1] If this meant the influence of the general notion of evolution, or even of the theory of organic evolution, the theme would be hopelessly vast. But, to a company of persons acquainted with the history of science, I am not likely to appear to be evading the responsibilities of my topic if I confine this paper chiefly to a consideration of the influence of the hypothesis

---

* Reprinted from *Bulletin of Washington University* (St. Louis, Mo.), April 1909, pp. 85–89, 91–99. Copyright 1909 by Washington University Publications. Used by permission of Washington University Publications.

[1] [The approach of the centenary of *The Origin of Species* revived interest in this subject and produced a number of interesting books and articles, including the following: William Irvine, *Apes, Angels, and Victorians* (New York: McGraw-Hill Book Company, 1955); Loren Eiseley, *Darwin's Century* (Garden City: Doubleday & Company, 1958); John Greene, *The Death of Adam: Evolution and Its Impact on Western Thought* (Ames: Iowa State University Press, 1959); and Gertrude Himmelfarb, *Darwin and the Darwinian Revolution* (Garden City: Doubleday & Company, 1959). Donald Fleming examines some of the most recent literature in his review article "The Centenary of the *Origin of Species*," in *Journal of the History of Ideas*, June–Sept. 1959, pp. 437–446.]

of natural selection upon the philosophical and religious reflection of the last fifty years.

In the theory of the transformation of species there is nothing distinctively Darwinian. Darwin was not the first to promulgate that theory; he was not the first to make it widely familiar to students of geology and zoology; he was not even the first to defend it by clear and reasonably cogent arguments—though no one, it is true, had, before the *Origin of Species,* presented the evidence with such thoroughness and with such a masterly array of scrupulously verified specific data. The theory itself had been enunciated by the middle of the 18th century, and by men of distinction among the scientists of the period—by a president of the Berlin Academy of Science and by the editor of the *Encyclopédie.*[2] At that time the evidence in its favor was, perhaps, scarcely overwhelming. But the succeeding century was marked by a series of great discoveries in comparative anatomy, in embryology, above all in geology and paleontology, which converged so perfectly upon a single conclusion, that by the 1840's the theory of transformation may be said to have been an actually established, though not a generally accepted scientific hypothesis. It was, in fact, adopted by a number of men of intellectual eminence in Darwin's own generation—some of them naturalists, some of them philosophical followers of the general progress of the sciences—long before the famous meeting of the Linnean Society in 1858.[3] Among these were such diverse minds as E. Geoffroy St. Hilaire, Robert Chambers, Wallace, Spencer, von Baer, Emerson, Charles Kingsley, and Tennyson. The supposition of the immutability of species had simply become untenable for any clear-thinking and scientifically well-informed mind not hobbled by theological dogmas. The only hypothesis, other than that of evolution, which the existing state of geological and zoological knowledge in 1850 made possible at all was the amazing one in which the great Agassiz[4] took refuge, and which was taught in the college text-books at that time. According to this hypothesis the Deity had created different immutable species by fits and starts, strewing them at irregular intervals along the vast reaches of geologic time; he had permitted the great majority of these to become extinct under the operation of ordinary natural causes, and had then been obliged to replace them with fresh creations, not al-

---

[2] [The reference is to Denis Diderot's theory of "transformism."]

[3] [The meeting at which Darwin's theory was presented publicly for the first time, together with a paper by Alfred Russel Wallace outlining a similar theory.]

[4] [The Swiss-American naturalist Louis Agassiz (1807–1873).]

ways markedly superior in type to their unfortunate precursors; in these later-formed creatures he had frequently reproduced organs useful and important in the earlier types but now redundant and purposeless —like the proverbial Japanese tailor, who faithfully copies all the holes, wrinkles, and stains in the discarded European garment given him as a model. The Creator, moreover (as Agassiz, in particular, insisted), had implanted in the higher forms the curious but entirely meaningless habit of briefly recapitulating, in the embryonic stages of their development, the sequence of extinct organic forms that had succeeded one another in earlier geological periods. This account of the origin of species had, assuredly, in the highest possible degree all the vices of which a scientific hypothesis is capable; and it was, though cherished in the name of orthodoxy, as irreligious as it was fantastic. The doctrine of immutability, in short, though it kept up for a while a brave show of fight, was really a desperately wounded creature fifteen or twenty years before Darwin openly attacked it. It had not been he who first gave chase, and it was not he who dealt it the deep thrusts that were sure in any case to prove fatal. He merely gave it, with the composure and deftness of a great master of the hunt, its *coup de grâce*. The situation about the middle of the century is clearly indicated by Spencer's [5] remark upon a paper of his in defence of the development theory, published in 1852. By this time, he observes, "the belief in organic evolution had taken deep root and drawn to itself a large amount of evidence—evidence not derived from numerous special instances, but derived from the general aspects of organic nature and from *the necessity of accepting the hypothesis of evolution when the hypothesis of special creation (i.e., the creation of species ready-made, separately, and at successive periods) had been rejected.* The special creation belief had dropped out of my mind many years before, and I could not remain in a suspended state; acceptance of the only possible alternative was peremptory." (*Life and Letters,* II, p. 317.)

The distinctive influence of Darwin upon modern thought is, then, properly speaking, the influence of the doctrine of natural selection. This itself is too large a theme to be even fairly opened up, in the time available on this occasion; any sort of serious discussion of it is beyond the question. Some tendencies of the doctrine that have been historically manifest—when its correctness is assumed, and it is carried over from technical biology to serve in the general interpretation of

[5] [Herbert Spencer (1820–1903).]

nature and in the guidance of human life—may perhaps be roughly indicated.

1. *Darwinism and Teleology.* Natural selection was conceived by Darwin to be not only the dominant factor in the explanation of the *how* of evolution, but also in the explanation of the *how* of adaptation. The idea of adaptation loomed very large in his mind; the essence of his doctrine—and its essential error, in the opinion of T. H. Morgan and other contemporary biologists—is the view that all organic evolution consists in progressive adaptation to environment, and that accordingly the principal causes of the appearance of new species and the causes of adaptation are one and the same. Now, there had flourished for some time before Darwin a class of writers whose minds had also been obsessed with the fact of adaptation—namely the writers upon natural theology of the 18th and early 19th century; in the existence of adaptations they had found an argument for a sort of optimistic and anthropomorphic theism, which had reached its most elaborate and monumental expression in a series of monographs, the *Bridgewater Treatises,* published between 1830 and 1840, written by men of high scientific reputation, such as Whewell, Sir Charles Bell, Buckland, and Kirby. There are certain curious connections between Darwin and the *Bridgewater Treatises;* and one may find a sort of historic irony in the circumstance that the first words after the title in the *Origin of Species* are a motto taken from one of those treatises. For, on the one hand, the characteristic excess of Darwinism, if there be such, is its exaggerated preoccupation with just that aspect of nature with which the arguers from design had been so much preoccupied; and on the other hand, the doctrine of natural selection, in so far as it gained acceptance, was the death sentence of all arguments from design based upon the consideration of organic adaptations. To the rigorous logician, indeed, there had always been an obvious fallacy in the argument from adaptations, as an effect, to supernatural agency and conscious, beneficent purpose, as their cause. The fallacy has been called that of "transcendent inference"; from knowing, through experience, that certain effects are caused only by purposive human agency, we have no ground whatever for concluding that certain other effects, of whose causation we have had no experience at all, must be due to non-human purposive agency. The argument, as Clifford observed in criticizing a later and non-biological variant of the teleological proof of intelligent agency in nature, is neither more nor less cogent than the following: "Because the sea is salt and will put out a fire, there must have once been a fire at the

bottom of it. This can only have been effected by the agency of the whale who lives in the middle of Sahara." But this purely negative objection to the design argument was always more sound in logic than effective in persuasion. All that it really said was that experience does not show us *whether or not* adaptations are due to non-mechanistic, purposive agency. Darwin, however, came forward with a theory whereby virtually all adaptations were declared to be positively explicable without any invocation of teleology, blind or conscious—to be explicable as the results of a purely mechanical sort of necessity. Given promiscuous variability of all organisms in all directions—given, also, a struggle between them for existence—and they are forced and squeezed, by the natural conditions of that struggle, into increasing adaptation. Darwin himself, modest and reluctant as he was to express himself upon religious questions, noted this theological consequence of his doctrine. He says in his *Autobiography*: "The old argument from design in nature . . . which once seemed to me so conclusive, fails, now that the law of natural selection has been discovered. We can no longer argue that, for instance, the beautiful hinge of a bivalve shell must have been made by an intelligent being, like the hinge of a door by a man. There seems to be no more design in the variability of organic beings, and in the action of natural selection, than in the course which the wind blows." (*Life and Letters of Charles Darwin*, I, p. 279.)

The appearance and diffusion of the natural selection doctrine was thus an important episode in the movement of modern thought away from teleological explanations of natural processes and towards a statement of the law of occurrence of all such processes in consistently mechanistic terms. . . .

To sum up this part of the subject, then: teleological ideas long had their special stronghold in biology; they chiefly took the form of an emphasis upon adaptations; this emphasis Darwin inherited, but he robbed the fact of adaptation of any teleological import, by indicating the possibility of a purely mechanistic explanation of it. He thus closed a chapter in both biology and natural theology. Teleology is now revived in a new phase; but, as a result of Darwin's influence, it no longer figures as an argument from design or contrivance, and it is not interested in the adaptive aspects of organisms. The teleologists of to-day are concerned to prove the distinctiveness and autonomy of the vital process, in contrast with mechanical processes; they are not concerned to exhibit the inevitable interadjustment of the parts of Nature as evidence of the inventive ingenuity of a Divine Artificer.

2. *Darwinism and Pessimism*. Nothing in the prevalent world-view of a generation of men is of more practical significance than the degree of its confidence in the rationality, meaningfulness, and congeniality to man's ideals, of the external universe and its general modes of behavior. In this respect Darwin's influence has been of an extremely mixed character. As the most effective of the promoters of evolutionist views in biology, he has been also a promoter of cheerfulness and optimism; but as the author of the hypothesis of natural selection he has seemed to give a sort of scientific version of the melancholy picture of the nature of things drawn by Schopenhauer forty years earlier.[6] No one can deny that the general theory of cosmic, organic, and social evolution has provided later 19th century thought with a superior substitute for that species of static optimism prevailing in the 18th century—that persuasion that this is demonstrably "the best of possible worlds" which Voltaire ridiculed in *Candide*. It has been still more agreeable and encouraging to believe that the world is so constituted that it inevitably proeeds from lower to higher, from worse to better. This bland evolutional optimism has become a sort of religion with many, especially with the liberal schools of theologians; it has found in Mr. John Fiske its most popular prophet. But when you turn from evolution itself to the Darwinian conception of the way in which evolution has chiefly been brought about, you come upon a very different story. The doctrine of natural selection represents Nature as a scene of monstrous waste and of universal conflict, a veritable *bellum omnium contra omnes*. It pictures the teeming Universal Mother as reckless in the production of aspirants for life, but strangely parsimonious in her provision of the means of maintaining life—leaving to every one of the hungry children at her board only the privilege of snatching the food of his neighbors, only the grim alternative of destroying or being destroyed. It declares these three unlovely aspects of the world—its wastefulness, its disharmony, and its cruelty—to be not simply casual details of the picture, but the very essence of that whole evolutional process which, regarded in its results and not in its methods, had seemed so admirable and so edifying to contemplate. These aspects of Nature had been pointed out by Tennyson in a famous passage of *In Memoriam* written fifteen years before the appearance of the *Origin of*

[6] [As noted in the Introduction, later evolutionists have drawn a less melancholy picture. See, for instance, Julian Huxley, *The Uniqueness of Man* (London: Chatto & Windus, 1941); and Pierre Teilhard de Chardin, *The Phenomenon of Man* (New York: Harper and Brothers, 1959).]

Species; but made, as they were by Darwin, the central and explanatory facts in the entire scheme of organic existence, they became yet more monstrous to the imagination by coming to seem more universal and more systematic. "Man," as Mr. Chesterton [7] has put it, with characteristic point, if also with characteristic rhetorical excess: "Man had been engaged through innumerable ages in a struggle with sin. . . . But in this struggle he had always had nature on his side. He might be polluted and agonized, but the flowers were innocent and the hills were strong." But the beginning of the spread of the Darwinian theory was "an hour when to all mortal appearance the whole of the physical world deserted to the devil. The universe, governed by violence and death, left man to fight alone, with a handful of myths and memories. Men had to wander in polluted fields and lift their eyes to abominable hills. They had to arm themselves against the cruelty of flowers and the crimes of the grass." Something of this sort, assuredly, Darwinism tended to suggest to the imagination of men as they looked out upon nature: and in so far as it did so, it was one of the factors contributing to the later nineteenth century manifestations of ' pessimism. No one, I hope, will understand me to mean by this that Darwin himself was a preacher of pessimism. Such questions lay for the most part beyond the range of his discussion; his business was to describe facts and devise scientific hypotheses for the explanation of them. In the one passage known to me in which he deals with the bearings of his doctrine upon the issue raised by the pessimists, he argues to the conclusion that the natural selection theory requires us to suppose that there is more pleasure than suffering in the world of sentient organisms—chiefly on the ground that pain, if long continued, tends to diminished vitality and efficiency in action, and cannot, therefore, have been a frequent concomitant of the discharge of ordinary functions in species destined to survival. This manifestly ignores the fact that, upon the Darwinian assumption of the extreme intensity of the struggle for existence, the greater number of *individuals* are *not* destined to survive long, or to develop normally and unimpededly their ordinary functions. And in any case, the doctrine of a universal struggle for existence has led to melancholy views of the relation of nature to human ideals, not merely because of the quantity of suffering involved in the struggle, but because if its wastefulness and indirectness as . a means of bringing evolution about, and because of the spectacle of disharmony and violence which

[7] [Gilbert Chesterton (1874–1936), noted English literary critic and author.]

it presents. It has, indeed, always been possible to point out the other side of the shield: if natural selection means that all progress comes by means of struggle and ruthless elimination of individuals and species, it also means that struggle and elimination carry forward progress. But this consideration does not relieve the situation so much as has sometimes been imagined. For adaptation and progress (in any ethical or aesthetic sense) are not universally synonymous; and in any case, the end attained does not justify nor render any more edifying the means. As George Eliot observed:

> It had not much
> Consoled the race of mastodons to know
> Their forms would quicken with the elephant;
> They were not elephants, but mastodons.

Or as Huxley [8] still more pointedly expresses it: "It is not clear what compensation the *Eohippus* gets for his sorrows in the fact that, some millions of years afterwards, one of his descendants wins the Derby." When all is said, then, Nature, if viewed through the lenses of the Darwinian theory, is less likely to seem to the reflective mind what Wordsworth professed to find it:

> The anchor of my purest thoughts, the nurse,
> The guide, the guardian of my heart, and soul
> Of all my moral being.

The aspects of Nature which the natural selection hypothesis brings into relief are in any event, it is true, real aspects, which might have been, and often were, recognized as such long before Darwin. Whether they are such centrally significant and ubiquitous aspects as Darwinism would make them out to be, is a question which contemporary biology is diligently endeavoring to settle by its own proper methods. One can only say now that the dominant tendency is distinctly towards an answer in the negative.

3. *Darwinism and Ethics*. Prolixity cannot be regarded as a favorable variation in participants in public exercises—though it is perhaps a signal instance of one tending to survive in spite of its unfavorableness. I may not, therefore, attempt more than a very brief indication of the real or supposed manifestations of Darwinism in ethics—the applications made of the principle of natural selection to the guidance of human behavior. The ethical teaching of Nietzsche is frequently represented as the most thoroughgoing and influential expression of Darwinism in

[8] [Thomas Henry Huxley (1825–1895), sometimes called "Darwin's Bulldog."]

morals; one of Nietzsche's principal expounders has declared him to
have been the first to deduce consistently the lessons of the Darwinian
theory for the conduct of life. But, as M. Fouillée has shown, the
relationship is more imaginary than real. While Nietzsche makes
struggle and conflict the highest good, it is *not* a struggle for life enforced by external conditions, a scramble of hard-pressed beings to
avoid starvation by the utilization of adaptive modifications. Nature,
for Nietzsche, is not niggardly, but prodigal and abounding in resources;
and the struggle which he finds everywhere—and finds good—is the
consequence of the overflowing energy and insatiable impulse to
activity of well-fed creatures, who fight because they cannot otherwise
express the sense of power and mastery that is in them. The idea that
vital activity is chiefly an affair of passive adaptation to environment is,
says Nietzsche, the idea of a neurasthenic. Thus natural selection and
the play of the *Wille zur Macht* have very little in common. More truly
Darwinian in ancestry—though wholly remote from Darwin's own
thought—is the "natural history view of mankind" and of the duty of
nations, expressed not many years ago by Mr. Karl Pearson.[9] This view
holds that a nation should be "kept up to a high pitch of external
efficiency by contest, chiefly by way of war with inferior races, and with
equal races by the struggle for trade routes and for the sources of food
supply." Above all, the inferior races must be quietly but firmly elim-
inated, in order that those capable of a higher civilization may enter
into their heritage. "When," says Mr. Pearson, "the struggle for existence
between races is suspended, the solution of great problems may be
unnaturally postponed; instead of the slow, stern processes of evolution,
cataclysmal solutions are prepared for the future. . . . This dependence
of progress on the survival of the fitter race, terribly black as it may
seem" (the reader will misapprehend Mr. Pearson if he takes the
antecedent of "black" to be "fitter race") "gives the struggle for existence
its redeeming features; it is the fiery crucible out of which comes the
finer metal. You may hope for the time when the sword shall be turned
into the ploughshare, when American and German and English traders
shall no longer compete in the markets of the world for their raw
material and for their food supply, when the white man and the dark
shall share the soil between them and each till as he lists. But . . .
when that day comes, mankind will no longer progress; there will be
nothing to check the fertility of inferior stock; the relentless law of

[9] *National Life from the Standpoint of Science*, 1901.

heredity will not be controlled and guided by natural selection (sic). Man will stagnate; and, unless he ceases to multiply, the catastrophe will come again; famine and pestilence, as we see them in the East, physical selection, instead of the struggle of race against race, will do the work more relentlessly, and, to judge from India and China, far less efficiently than of old."

Thus the political ethics of imperialism has presented itself to some scientifically trained minds as a natural inference from Darwin's biology; and there can be no doubt that the vogue of Darwinian ideas during the last quarter of the 19th century has been one potent factor making for the growth of the imperialistic temper among the *soi-disant* superior races. This sort of thing is, of course, no *necessary* inference from any principle of Darwin's;—both for the general reason that no ethical conclusion can be deduced with necessity from purely biological premises, and also for the special reason that, as experience shows, imperialism and militarism have a tendency to make the superior races who consciously "go in for" them very much less superior, both in a moral and in a biological sense. More convincing is the application of Darwinism to the internal problems of national development, which Mr. Pearson and many others, biologists and sociologists, have made. Given an end generally admitted to be desirable, and biology may indicate the measures necessary for its realization. There is a general agreement that certain evils still persist in civilized society which are largely due to physical heredity. And it may eventually prove that the most lasting and profound influence of Darwinism upon practice will come through its indirect suggestion of the necessity of applying a more rigorous process of selection to the human breed. . . .

These three aspects of Darwin's influence upon ethics which I have noted have all been ethical tendencies which, in Professor James' phrase, "make a difference"—affect definitely men's views towards concrete, practical issues. Meanwhile, beginning with Darwin himself, there has been a long succession of ethical theories that have consisted largely in translating the ordinary and generally accepted moral code into Darwinian categories. Taking the social aggregate rather than the individual as a unit, such theories have exhibited the familiar social virtues and the approved modes of behavior as requisites for the survival and efficiency of such a unit. The most important example of this type of ethical system, the *Science of Ethics* of Sir Leslie Stephen,[10]

[10] [Sir Leslie Stephen (1832–1904), famous English agnostic and man of letters.]

resorting to histology for the analogy which serves as its foundation, represents a race or a nation as made up of a sort of social tissue. In the long run, those races whose social tissue is the strongest will flourish best and will become predominant. The moral law is simply the definition of the qualities of healthy social tissue; and these qualities depend chiefly upon a high development, among the members of society, of the feeling of sympathy and the habit of acting with a view to the greatest happiness of the entire group. In Stephen's, as in most kindred ethical doctrines—in Spencer's for example—there is a fusion of two not altogether congenial elements—of evolutional, and specifically Darwinian, ideas with surviving influences from pre-Darwinian English utilitarianism. But even apart from the difficulties due to this entanglement, we are beginning, I think, to recognize that the effort to cram the moral ideas of civilized man into the rigid mould of the natural selection hypothesis is an artificial and not very promising enterprise. Here, too, it is becoming apparent that natural selection can play only a negative role; that while it checks all too widely aberrant variations, it does not account for all the wide range of modes of feeling and activity possible in so complex a thing as human nature, and does not of itself indicate any ground for preferring one such "survivable" mode over another. "Conduct adapted to promote the survival and biological efficiency of the social organism"—this has proven, unquestionably, an instructive and stimulating ethical formula, during the past generation; but it is not likely to be permanently accepted by mankind as an adequate summary of all the Law and the Prophets.

FREUD AND THE FUTURE *

Thomas Mann †

We are gathered here to do honour to a great scientist.[1] And the
question may very properly be raised: what justifies a man of letters
in assuming the role of spokesman on such an occasion? Or, passing on
the responsibility to the members of the learned society which chose
him, why should they not have selected one of their own kind, a man
of science, rather than an author, to celebrate in words the birthday of
their master? For an author, my friends, is a man essentially not bent
upon science, upon knowing, distinguishing, and analysing; he stands
for smple creation, for doing and making, and thus may be the object
of useful cognition, without, by his very nature having any competence
in it as subject. . . .

Be that as it may, the choice of an artist as the encomiast of a great
scientist is a comment upon both. In the first place, one deduces from
it a connection between the man of genius we now honour and the
world of creative literature; in the second place, it displays the peculiar
relations between the writer and the field of science whose declared and
acknowledged master and creator the other is. Now, the unique and
remarkable thing about this mutual close relation is that it remained
for so long unconscious—that is, in that region of the soul which we
have learned to call the unconscious, a realm whose discovery and

---

* Reprinted from *Essays of Three Decades* by Thomas Mann, pp. 411-417,
419, 427-428, by permission of Alfred A. Knopf, Inc. Copyright 1937 by Alfred
A. Knopf, Inc., and by permission of Martin Secker & Warburg Limited, London.

† Thomas Mann, one of Germany's great writers of the twentieth century, is
renowned for novels such as *Buddenbrooks* and *The Magic Mountain,* and also
well known for his learned essays on literary and intellectual figures.

[1] [Books on Freud and the Freudian Revolution are legion. The following are
substantial and provocative: Benjamin Nelson (ed.), *Freud and the 20th Century*
(New York: Meridian Books, Inc., 1957); Philip Rieff, *Freud: The Mind of the
Moralist* (New York: Viking Press, Inc., 1959); Norman O. Brown, *Life against
Death. The Psychoanalytical Meaning of History* (Middletown: Wesleyan Uni-
versity Press, 1959); Bruce Mazlish (ed.), *Psychoanalysis and History* (Engle-
wood Cliffs, N. J.: Prentice-Hall, 1963). See also related works by Calvin S.
Hall and Gardner Lindzey, *Theories of Personality* (New York: John Wiley &
Sons, Inc., 1957); and Ira Progoff, *The Death and Rebirth of Psychology* (New
York: Julian Press, 1956).]

investigation, whose conquest for humanity, are precisely the task and
mission of the wise genius whose fame we celebrate.[2] The close relation
between literature and psychoanalysis has been known for a long time
to both sides. But the solemn significance of this hour lies, at least in
my eyes and as a matter of personal feeling, in that on this evening
there is taking place the first official meeting between the two spheres,
in the acknowledgment and demonstration of their relationship.

I repeat that the profound sympathy between the two spheres had
existed for a long time unperceived. Actually we know that Sigmund
Freud, that mighty spirit in whose honour we are gathered together,
founder of psychoanalysis as a general method of research and as a
therapeutic technique, trod the steep path alone and independently, as
physician and natural scientist, without knowing that reinforcement
and encouragement lay to his hand in literature. He did not know
Nietzsche, scattered throughout whose pages one finds premonitory
flashes of truly Freudian insight; he did not know Novalis, whose
romantic-biologic fantasies so often approach astonishingly close to
analytic conceptions; he did not know Kierkegaard, whom he must
have found profoundly sympathetic and encouraging for the Christian
zeal which urged him on to psychological extremes; and, finally, he did
not know Schopenhauer, the melancholy symphonist of a philosophy
of the instinct, groping for change and redemption. Probably it must
be so. By his unaided effort, without knowledge of any previous
intuitive achievement, he had methodically to follow out the line of
his own researches; the driving force of his activity was probably increased by this very freedom from special advantage. And we think of
him as solitary—the attitude is inseparable from our earliest picture of
the man. Solitary in the sense of the word used by Nietzsche in that
ravishing essay "What is the Meaning of Ascetic Ideals?" when he
characterizes Schopenhauer as "a genuine philosopher, a self-poised
mind, a man and gallant knight, stern-eyed, with the courage of his
own strength, who knows how to stand alone and not wait on the beck
and nod of superior officers." In this guise of man and gallant knight,
a knight between Death and the Devil, I have been used to picture to
myself our psychologist of the unconscious, ever since his figure first
swam into my mental ken.

That happened late—much later than one might have expected,

[2] [Strictly speaking, of course, Freud did not "discover" the unconscious. On
this point see the pioneer work by Lancelot Law Whyte, *The Unconscious before
Freud* (New York: Basic Books, Inc., 1960).]

considering the connection between this science and the poetic and
creative impulse in general and mine in particular. . . .

I realized this connection only at a time when his achievement was
no longer thought of as merely a therapeutic method, whether recognized
or disputed; when it had long since outgrown his purely medical
implications and become a world movement which penetrated into every
field of science and every domain of the intellect: literature, the history
of art, religion and prehistory; mythology, folklore, pedagogy, and what
not—thanks to the practical and constructive zeal of experts who erected
a structure of more general investigation round the psychiatric and
medical core. Indeed, it would be too much to say that I came to psychoanalysis. It came to me. Through the friendly interest that some
younger workers in the field had shown in my work, from *Little Herr
Friedemann* to *Death in Venice, The Magic Mountain,* and the *Joseph*
novels, it gave me to understand that in my way I "belonged"; it made
me aware, as probably behoved it, of my own latent, preconscious
sympathies; and when I began to occupy myself with the literature of
psychoanalysis I recognized, arrayed in the ideas and the language of
scientific exactitude, much that had long been familiar to me through
my youthful mental experiences.

Perhaps you will kindly permit me to continue for a while in this
autobiographical strain, and not take it amiss if instead of speaking of
Freud I speak of myself. And indeed I scarcely trust myself to speak
about him. What new thing could I hope to say? But I shall also,
quite explicitly, be speaking in his honour in speaking of myself, in
telling you how profoundly and peculiarly certain experiences decisive
for my development prepared me for the Freudian experience. More
than once, and in many places, I have confessed to the profound, even
shattering impression made upon me as a young man by contact with
the philosophy of Arthur Schopenhauer, to which then a monument
was erected in the pages of *Buddenbrooks*. Here first, in the pessimism
of a metaphysics already very strongly equipped on the natural-science
side, I encountered the dauntless zeal for truth that stands for the
moral aspect of the psychology of the unconscious. This metaphysics,
in obscure revolt against centuries-old beliefs, preached the primacy of
the instinct over mind and reason; it recognized the will as the core
and the essential foundation of the world, in man as in all other
created beings; and the intellect as secondary and accidental, servant
of the will and its pale illuminant. This it preached not in malice, not
in the anti-human spirit of the mind-hostile doctrines of today, but in

the stern love of truth characteristic of the century which combated
idealism out of love for the ideal. It was so sincere, that nineteenth
century, that—through the mouth of Ibsen—it pronounced the lie, the
lies of life, to be indispensable. Clearly there is a vast difference whether
one assents to a lie out of sheer hatred of truth and the spirit or for the
sake of that spirit, in bitter irony and anguished pessimism! Yet the
distinction is not clear to everybody today.

Now, Freud, the psychologist of the unconscious, is a true son of the
century of Schopenhauer and Ibsen—he was born in the middle of it.
How closely related is his revolution to Schopenhauer's, not only in its
content, but also in its moral attitude! His discovery of the great role
played by the unconscious, the id, in the soul-life of man challenged
and challenges classical psychology, to which the consciousness and
the psyche are one and the same, as offensively as once Schopenhauer's
doctrine of the will challenged philosophical belief in reason and the
intellect. Certainly the early devotee of *The World as Will and Idea*
is at home in the admirable essay that is included in Freud's *New
Introductory Essays in Psychoanalysis* under the title "The Anatomy
of the Mental Personality." It describes the soul-world of the unconscious, the id, in language as strong, and at the same time in as
coolly intellectual, objective, and professional a tone, as Schopenhauer
might have used to describe his sinister kingdom of the will. "The
domain of the id," he says, is the dark, inaccessible part of our personality; the little that we know of it we have learned through the
study of dreams and of the formation of neurotic symptoms." He depicts
it as a chaos, a melting-pot of seething excitations. The id, he thinks,
is, so to speak, open towards the somatic, and receives thence into itself
compulsions which there find psychic expression—in what substratum
is unknown. From these impulses it receives its energy; but it is not
organized, produces no collective will, merely the striving to achieve
satisfaction for the impulsive needs operating under the pleasure
principle. In it no laws of thought are valid, and certainly not the law
of opposites. "Contradictory stimuli exist alongside each other without
cancelling each other out or even detracting from each other; at most
they unite in compromise forms under the compulsion of the controlling
economy for the release of energy." You perceive that this is a situation
which, in the historical experience of our own day, can take the upper
hand with ego, with a whole mass-ego, thanks to a moral devastation
which is produced by worship of the unconscious, the glorification of
its dynamic as the only life-promoting force, the systematic glorification

of the primitive and irrational.[3] For the unconscious, the id, is primitive and irrational, is pure dynamic. It knows no values, no good or evil, no morality. It even knows no time, no temporal flow, nor any effect of time upon its psychic process. "Wish stimuli," says Freud, "which have never overpassed the id, and impressions which have been repressed into its depths, are virtually indestructible, they survive decade after decade as though they had just happened. They can only be recognized as belonging to the past, devalued and robbed of their charge of energy, by becoming conscious through the analytic procedure." And he adds that therein lies pre-eminently the healing effect of analytic treatment. We perceive accordingly how antipathetic deep analysis must be to an ego that is intoxicated by a worship of the unconscious to the point of being in a condition of subterranean dynamic. It is only too clear and understandable that such an ego is deaf to analysis and that the name of Freud must not be mentioned in its hearing.

As for the ego itself, its situation is pathetic, well-nigh alarming. It is an alert, prominent, and enlightened little part of the id—much as Europe is a small and lively province of the greater Asia. The ego is that part of the id which became modified by contact with the outer world; equipped for the reception and preservation of stimuli; comparable to the integument with which any piece of living matter surrounds itself. A very perspicuous biological picture. Freud writes indeed a very perspicuous prose, he is an artist of thought, like Schopenhauer, and like him a writer of European rank. The relation with the outer world is, he says, decisive for the ego, it is the ego's task to represent the world to the id—for its good! For without regard for the superior power of the outer world the id, in its blind striving towards the satisfaction of its instincts, would not escape destruction. The ego takes cognizance of the outer world, it is mindful, it honourably tries to distinguish the objectively real from whatever is an accretion from its inward sources of stimulation. It is entrusted by the id with the lever of action; but between the impulse and the action it has interposed the delay of the thought-process, during which it summons experience to its aid and thus possesses a certain regulative superiority over the pleasure principle which rules supreme in the unconscious, correcting it by means of the principle of reality. But even so, how feeble it is! Hemmed in between the unconscious, the outer world, and what Freud calls the super-ego, it leads a pretty nervous and anguished existence.

[3] [The "moral devastation" to which Mann here refers is the Nazi movement in Germany.]

Its own dynamic is rather weak. It derives its energy from the id and in general has to carry out the latter's behests. It is fain to regard itself as the rider and the unconscious as the horse. But many a time it is ridden by the unconscious; and I take leave to add what Freud's rational morality prevents him from saying, that under some circumstances it makes more progress by this illegitimate means.

But Freud's description of the id and the ego—is it not to a hair Schopenhauer's description of the Will and the Intellect, a translation of the latter's metaphysics into psychology? So he who had been initiated into the metaphysics of Schopenhauer and in Nietzsche tasted the painful pleasure of psychology—he must needs have been filled with a sense of recognition and familiarity when first, encouraged thereto by its denizens, he entered the realms of psychoanalysis and looked about him. . . .

Perhaps this is the moment, my friends, to indulge on this festive occasion in a little polemic against Freud himself. He does not esteem philosophy very highly. His scientific exactitude does not permit him to regard it as a science. He reproaches it with imagining that it can present a continuous and consistent picture of the world; with over-estimating the objective value of logical operations; with believing in intuitions as a source of knowledge and with indulging in positively animistic tendencies, in that it believes in the magic of words and the influence of thought upon reality. But would philosophy really be thinking too highly of itself on these assumptions? Has the world ever been changed by anything save by thought and its magic vehicle the Word? I believe that in actual fact philosophy ranks before and above the natural sciences and that all method and exactness serve its intuitions and its intellectual and historical will. In the last analysis it is always a matter of the *quod erat demonstrandum*. Scientific freedom from assumptions is or should be a moral fact. But intellectually it is, as Freud points out, probably an illusion. One might strain the point and say that science has never made a discovery without being authorized and encouraged thereto by philosophy. . . .

And now this word "future": I have used it in the title of my address, because it is this idea, the idea of the future, that I involuntarily like best to connect with the name of Freud. But even as I have been speaking I have been asking myself whether I have not been guilty of a cause of confusion; whether—from what I have said up to now—a better title might not have been something like "Freud and the Myth." And yet I rather cling to the combination of name and word and I should like to justify and make clear its relation to what I have so far said. I make bold to believe that in that novel so kin to the Freudian world, making as it does the light of psychology play upon the myth,[4] there lie hidden seeds and elements of a new and coming sense of our humanity. And no less firmly do I hold that we shall one day recognize in Freud's life-work the cornerstone for the building of a new anthropology and therewith of a new structure, to which many stones are being brought up today, which shall be the future dwelling of a wiser and freer humanity. This physicianly psychologist will, I make no doubt at all, be honoured as the path-finder towards a humanism of the future, which we dimly divine and which will have experienced much that the earlier humanism knew not of. It will be a humanism standing in a different relation to the powers of the lower world, the unconscious, the id: a relation bolder, freer, blither, productive of a riper art than any possible in our neurotic, fear-ridden, hate-ridden world. Freud is of the opinion that the significance of psychoanalysis as a science of the unconscious will in the future far outrank its value as a therapeutic method. But even as a science of the unconscious it is a therapeutic method, in the grand style, a method overarching the individual case. Call this, if you choose, a poet's utopia; but the thought is after all not unthinkable that the resolution of our great fear and our great hate, their conversion into a different relation to the unconscious which shall be more the artist's, more ironic and yet not necessarily irreverent, may one day be due to the healing effect of this very science.

The analytic revelation is a revolutionary force. With it a blithe scepticism has come into the world, a mistrust that unmasks all the schemes and subterfuges of our own souls. Once roused and on the alert, it cannot be put to sleep again. It infiltrates life, undermines its raw naïveté, takes from it the strain of its own ignorance, de-emotionalizes it, as it were, inculcates the taste for understatement, as the English call it—for the deflated rather than for the inflated word, for the cult which exerts its influence by moderation, by modesty. Modesty—what a beautiful word! In the German (*Bescheidenheit*) it originally had to do with knowing and only later got its present meaning; while the Latin word from which the English comes means a way of doing—in short, both together give us almost the sense of the French *savoir faire* —to know how to do. May we hope that this may be the fundamental

---

[4] [The novel of which Mann speaks is his own *Joseph and His Brothers* in which there is much talk about myth and the unconscious.]

temper of that more blithely objective and peaceful world which the science of the unconscious may be called to usher in?

Its mingling of the pioneer with the physicianly spirit justifies such a hope. Freud once called his theory of dreams "a bit of scientific new-found land won from superstition and mysticism." The word "won" expresses the colonizing spirit and significance of his work. "Where id was, shall be ego," he epigrammatically says. And he calls analysis a cultural labour comparable to the draining of the Zuider Zee. Almost in the end the traits of the venerable man merge into the lineaments of the grey-haired Faust, whose spirit urges him

> To shut the imperious sea from the shore away,
> Set narrower bounds to the broad water's waste.
>
> Then open I to many millions space
> Where they may live, not safe-secure, but free
> And active. And such a busy swarming I would see
> Standing amid free folk on a free soil.

The free folk are the people of a future freed from fear and hate, and ripe for peace.

THE ORIGINS AND SIGNIFICANCE OF THE EXISTENTIAL MOVEMENT IN PSYCHOLOGY *

Rollo May †

The first few pages of this chapter introduce what has come to be known in Europe and America as the "existential movement in psychology." This movement, associated with the names of Ludwig Binswanger in Switzerland, Rollo May in the United States, and others, represents an interesting combination of existential ideas with depth

* Reprinted from Rollo May, Ernest Angel, and Henri F. Ellenberger (eds.), *Existence. A New Dimension in Psychiatry and Psychology*, pp. 10–23, 34–36. Copyright 1958 by Basic Books, Inc. Used by permission of Basic Books, Inc.

† Rollo May is Professor of Clinical Psychology at New York University. His publications include *The Meaning of Anxiety* and a number of important articles on Existential Psychology.

psychology. The author then addresses himself to the question: What is Existentialism?

We must now remove a major stumbling block—namely, the confusion surrounding the term, "existentialism." [1] The word is bandied about to mean everything—from the posturing defiant dilettantism of some members of the *avant garde* on the Left Bank in Paris, to a philosophy of despair advocating suicide, to a system of anti-rationalist German thought written in a language so esoteric as to exasperate any empirically minded reader. Existentialism, rather, is an expression of profound dimensions of the modern emotional and spiritual temper and is shown in almost all aspects of our culture. It is found not only in psychology and philosophy but in art, *vide* Van Gogh, Cezanne, and Picasso—and in literature, *vide* Dostoevski, Baudelaire, Kafka, and Rilke. Indeed, in many ways it is the unique and specific portrayal of the psychological predicament of contemporary Western man. This cultural movement, as we shall see later in detail, has its roots in the same historical situation and the same psychological crises which called forth psychoanalysis and other forms of psychotherapy.

Confusions about the term occur even in usually highly literate places. *The New York Times,* in a report commenting on Sartre's denunciation of, and final break with, the Russian Communists for their suppression of freedom in Hungary, identified Sartre as a leader in "existentialism, a broadly materialistic form of thought." The report illustrates two reasons for the confusion—first, the identification of existentialism in the popular mind in this country with the writings of Jean-Paul Sartre. Quite apart from the fact that Sartre is known here for his dramas, movies, and novels rather than for his major, penetrating psychological analyses, it must be emphasized that he represents a nihilistic, subjectivist extreme in existentialism which invites misunderstanding, and his position is by no means the most useful introduction to the movement. But the second more serious confusion in the *Times* report is its definition of existentialism as "broadly materialistic." Noth-

---

[1] [The bibliography of Existentialism is by now formidable. For books and articles on the French Existentialists up to 1950, consult Kenneth Douglas, *A Critical Bibliography of Existentialism* (New Haven: Yale: French Studies, 1950). The following are good general studies: Paul Tillich, "Existential Philosophy," *Journal of the History of Ideas,* Jan. 1944; Marjorie Grene, *Dreadful Freedom* (Chicago: The University of Chicago Press, 1948); F. H. Heinemann, *Existentialism and the Modern Predicament* (New York: Harper & Brothers, 1953); William Barrett, *Irrational Man* (Garden City: Doubleday & Company, 1958).]

ing could be less accurate—nothing, unless it be the exact opposite, namely, describing it as an idealistic form of thinking. For the very essence of this approach is that it seeks to analyze and portray the human being—whether in art or literature or philosophy or psychology— on a level which undercuts the old dilemma of materialism versus idealism.

Existentialism, in short, is the endeavor to understand man by cutting below the cleavage between subject and object which has bedeviled Western thought and science since shortly after the Renaissance. This cleavage Binswanger[2] calls "the cancer of all psychology up to now . . . the cancer of the doctrine of subject-object cleavage of the world." The existential way of understanding human beings has some illustrious progenitors in Western history, such as Socrates in his dialogues, Augustine in his depth-psychological analyses of the self, Pascal in his struggle to find a place for the "heart's reasons which the reason knows not of." But it arose specifically just over a hundred years ago in Kierkegaard's violent protest against the reigning rationalism of his day, Hegel's "totalitarianism of reason," to use Maritain's phrase. Kierkegaard proclaimed that Hegel's identification of abstract truth with reality was an illusion and amounted to trickery. "Truth exists," wrote Kierkegaard, "only as the individual himself produces it in action." He and the existentialists following him protested firmly against the rationalists and idealists who would see man only as a subject—that is, as having reality only as a thinking being. But just as strongly they fought against the tendency to treat man as an object to be calculated and controlled, exemplified in the almost overwhelming tendencies in the Western world to make human beings into anonymous units to fit like robots into the vast industrial and political collectivisms of our day.

These thinkers sought the exact opposite of intellectualism for its own sake. They would have protested more violently than classical psychoanalysis against the use of thinking as a defense against vitality or as a substitute for immediate experience. One of the early existentialists of the sociological wing, Feuerbach, makes this appealing admonition, "Do not wish to be a philosopher in contrast to being a man . . . do not think as a thinker . . . think as a living, real being. Think in Existence."

The term "existence," coming from the root *ex-sistere*, means

[2] [Ludwig Binswanger (1881-   ), Swiss psychiatrist, author of many books on "Existential Psychology."]

literally to *stand out, to emerge.* This accurately indicates what these cultural representatives sought, whether in art or philosophy or psychology—namely, to portray the human being not as a collection of static substances or mechanisms or patterns but rather as emerging and becoming, that is to say, as existing. For no matter how interesting or theoretically true is the fact that I am composed of such and such chemicals or act by such and such mechanisms or patterns, the crucial question always is that I happen to exist at this given moment in time and space, and my problem is how I am to be aware of that fact and what I shall do about it. As we shall see later, the existential psychologists and psychiatrists do not at all rule out the study of dynamisms, drives, and patterns of behavior. But they hold that these cannot be understood in any given person except in the context of the overarching fact that here is a person who happens *to exist, to be,* and if we do not keep this in mind, all else we know about this person will lose its meaning. Thus their approach is always dynamic; existence refers to coming into being, becoming. Their endeavor is to understand this becoming not as a sentimental artifact but as the fundamental structure of human existence. When the term "being" is used in the following chapters, as it often is, the reader should remember that it is not a static word but a verb form, the participle of the verb "to be." Existentialism is basically concerned with *ontology,* that is, the science of being (*ontos,* from Greek "being").

We can see more clearly the significance of the term if we recall that traditionally in Western thought "existence" has been set over against "essence." Essence refers to the greenness of this stick of wood, let us say, and its density, weight, and other characteristics which give it substance. By and large Western thought since the Renaissance has been concerned with essences. Traditional science seeks to discover such essences or substances; it assumes an essentialist metaphysics, as Professor Wild of Harvard puts it.[3] The search for essences may indeed produce highly significant universal laws in science or brilliant abstract conceptualizations in logic or philosophy. But it can do this only by abstraction. The *existence* of the given individual thing has to be left out of the picture. For example, we can demonstrate that three apples added to three make six. But this would be just as true if we sub-

---

[3] John Wild, *The Challenge of Existentialism* (Bloomington: Indiana University Press, 1955). Modern physics, with Heisenberg, Bohr, and similar trends have changed at this point, paralleling, as we shall see later, one side of the existentialist development. We are talking above of the traditional ideas of Western science.

stituted unicorns for apples; it makes no difference to the mathematical truth of the proposition whether apples or unicorns actually exist or not. That is to say, a proposition can be *true* without being *real*. Perhaps just because this approach has worked so magnificently in certain areas of science, we tend to forget that it necessarily involves a detached viewpoint and that the living individual must be omitted. There remains the chasm between truth and reality. And the crucial question which confronts us in psychology and other aspects of the science of man is precisely this chasm between what is *abstractly true* and what is *existentially real* for the given living person.

Lest it seem that we are setting up an artificial, straw-man issue, let us point out that this chasm between truth and reality is openly and frankly admitted by sophisticated thinkers in behavioristic and conditioning psychology. Kenneth W. Spence, distinguished leader of one wing of behavior theory, writes, "The question of whether any particular realm of behavior phenomena is more real or closer to real life and hence should be given priority in investigation does not, or at least should not, arise for the psychologist *as scientist*." That is to say, it does not primarily matter whether what is being studied is real or not. What realms, then, should be selected for study? Spence gives priority to phenomena which lend themselves "to the degrees of control and analysis necessary for the formulation of abstract laws." Nowhere has our point been put more unabashedly and clearly—what can be reduced to *abstract laws* is selected, and whether what you are studying has reality or not is irrelevant to this goal. On the basis of this approach many an impressive system in psychology has been erected, with abstraction piled high upon abstraction—the authors succumbing, as we intellectuals are wont, to their "edifice complex"—until an admirable and imposing structure is built. The only trouble is that the edifice has more often than not been separated from human reality in its very foundations. Now the thinkers in the existential tradition hold the exact opposite to Spence's view, and so do the psychiatrists and psychologists in the existential psychotherapy movement. They insist that it is necessary and possible to have a science of man which studies human beings in their reality.

Kierkegaard, Nietzsche, and those who followed them accurately foresaw this growing split between truth and reality in Western culture, and they endeavored to call Western man back from the delusion that reality can be comprehended in an abstracted, detached way. But though they protested vehemently against arid intellectualism, they were by no means simple activists. Nor were they antirational. Anti-intellectualism and other movements in our day which make thinking subordinate to acting must not at all be confused with existentialism. Either alternative—making man subject *or* object—results in losing the living, existing person. Kierkegaard and the existential thinkers appealed to a reality *underlying both subjectivity and objectivity*. We must not only study a person's experience as such, they held, but even more we must study the man to whom the experience is happening, the one who is doing the experiencing. They insist, as Tillich puts it, that "Reality or Being is not the object of cognitive experience, but is rather 'existence,' is Reality as immediately experienced, with the accent on the inner, personal character of man's immediate experience." This comment, as well as several above, will indicate to the reader how close the existentialists are to present-day depth-psychology. It is by no means accidental that the greatest of them in the nineteenth century, Kierkegaard and Nietzsche, happen also to be among the most remarkable psychologists (in the dynamic sense) of all time and that one of the contemporary leaders of this school, Karl Jaspers, was originally a psychiatrist and wrote a notable text on psycho-pathology. When one reads Kierkegaard's profound analyses of anxiety and despair or Nietzsche's amazingly acute insights into the dynamics of resentment and the guilt and hostility which accompany repressed emotional powers, one must pinch himself to realize that he is reading works written seventy-five and a hundred years ago and not some new contemporary psychological analysis. The existentialists are centrally concerned with rediscovering the living person amid the compartmentalization and dehumanization of modern culture, and in order to do this they engage in depth psychological analysis. Their concern is not with isolated psychological reactions in themselves but rather with the psychological being of the living man who is doing the experiencing. That is to say, they use psychological terms with an ontological meaning.[4]

[4] For readers who wish more historical background, we append this note. In the winter of 1841, Schelling gave his famous series of lectures at the University of Berlin before a distinguished audience including Kierkegaard, Burckhardt, Engels, Bakunin. Schelling set out to overthrow Hegel, whose vast rationalist system, including, as we have said, the identification of abstract truth with reality and the bringing of all of history into an "absolute whole," held immense and dominant popularity in the Europe of the middle of the nineteenth century. Though many of Schelling's listeners were bitterly disappointed in his answers to Hegel, the existential movement may be said to have begun there. Kierkegaard went back to Denmark and in 1844 published his *Philosophical Fragments,* and

Martin Heidegger is generally taken as the fountainhead of present-day existential thought. His seminal work, *Being and Time,* was of radical importance in giving Binswanger and other existential psychiatrists and psychologists the deep and broad basis they sought for understanding man. Heidegger's thought is rigorous, logically incisive, and "scientific" in the European sense of pursuing with unrelenting vigor and thoroughness whatever implications his inquiries led him to. But his work is almost impossible to translate. Only a few essays are available in English.[5] Jean-Paul Sartre's best contributions to our subject are his phenomenological descriptions of psychological processes. In addition to Jaspers, other prominent existential thinkers are Gabriel Marcel in France, Nicolas Berdyaev, originally Russian but until his recent death a resident of Paris, and Ortega y Gasset and Unamuno in Spain. Paul Tillich shows the existential approach in his work, and in many ways his book *The Courage to Be* is the best and most cogent presentation of existentialism as an approach to actual living available in English.

The novels of Kafka portray the despairing, dehumanized situation in modern culture from which and to which existentialism speaks. *The Stranger* and *The Plague,* by Albert Camus, represent excellent examples in modern literature in which existentialism is partially self-conscious. But perhaps the most vivid of all portrayals of the meaning of existentialism is to be found in modern art, partly because it is articulated symbolically rather than as self-conscious thought and partly because art always reveals with special clarity the underlying spiritual and emotional temper of the culture. We shall frequently refer to the relation of modern

---

two years later he wrote the declaration of independence of existentialism, *Concluding Unscientific Postscript.* . . .

Then a new impetus came in the 1880's with the work of Dilthey, and particularly with Friedrich Nietzsche, the "philosophy of life" movement, and the work of Bergson.

The third and contemporary phase of existentialism came after the shock to the Western world caused by World War I. Kierkegaard and the early Marx were rediscovered, and the serious challenges to the spiritual and psychological bases of Western society given by Nietzsche could no longer be covered over by Victorian self-satisfied placidity. The specific form of this third phase owes much to the phenomenology of Edmund Husserl, which gave to Heidegger, Jaspers, and the others the tool they needed to undercut the subject-object cleavage which had been such a stumbling-block in science as well as philosophy. There is an obvious similarity between existentialism, in its emphasis on truth as produced in action, with the process philosophies, such as Whitehead's, and American pragmatism, particularly as in William James.

[5] [Since this chapter was written Heidegger's main work, *Being and Time,* has appeared in English translation.]

art and existentialism in the following pages. Here let us only note that some of the common elements in the work of such outstanding representatives of the modern movement as Van Gogh, Cezanne, and Picasso are, *first,* a revolt against the hypocritical academic tradition of the late nineteenth century, *second,* an endeavor to pierce below surfaces to grasp a new relation to the reality of nature, *third,* an endeavor to recover vitality and honest, direct aesthetic experience, and, *fourth,* the desperate attempt to express the immediate underlying meaning of the modern human situation, even though this means portraying despair and emptiness. Tillich, for example, holds that Picasso's painting "Guernica" gives the most gripping and revealing portrayal of the atomistic, fragmentized condition of European society which preceded World War II and "shows what is now in the souls of many Americans as disruptiveness, existential doubt, emptiness and meaninglessness."

The fact that the existential approach arose as an indigenous and spontaneous answer to crises in modern culture is shown not only in the fact that it emerged in art and literature but also in the fact that different philosophers in diverse parts of Europe often developed these ideas without conscious relation to each other. Though Heidegger's main work, *Being and Time,* was published in 1927, Ortega y Gasset already in 1924 had developed and partially published strikingly similar ideas without any direct knowledge of Heidegger's work.

It is true, of course, that existentialism had its birth in a time of cultural crisis, and it is always found in our day on the sharp revolutionary edge of modern art, literature, and thought. To my mind this fact speaks for the validity of its insights rather than the reverse. When a culture is caught in the profound convulsions of a transitional period, the individuals in the society understandably suffer spiritual and emotional upheaval; and finding that the accepted mores and ways of thought no longer yield security, they tend either to sink into dogmatism and conformism, giving up awareness, or are forced to strive for a heightened self-consciousness by which to become aware of their existence with new conviction and on new bases. This is one of the most important affinities of the existential movement with psychotherapy—both are concerned with individuals in crisis. And far from saying that the insights of a crisis period are "simply the product of anxiety and despair," we are more likely to find, as we do time and again in psychoanalysis, that a crisis is exactly what is required to shock people out of unaware dependence upon external dogma and to force them to unravel layers of pretense to reveal naked truth about themselves which, however unpleasant, will at least be solid. Existentialism is an attitude which accepts man as always becoming, which means potentially in crisis. But this does not mean it will be despairing. Socrates, whose dialectical search for truth in the individual is the prototype of existentialism, was optimistic. But this approach is understandably more apt to appear in ages of transition, when one age is dying and the new one not yet born, and the individual is either homeless and lost or achieves a new self-consciousness. . . .

We shall now look at the remarkable parallel between the problems of modern man to which the existentialists on one hand and psychoanalysts on the other devote themselves. From different perspectives and on different levels, both analyze anxiety, despair, alienation of man from himself and his society.

Freud describes the neurotic personality of the late nineteenth century as one suffering from fragmentation, that is, from repression of instinctual drives, blocking off of awareness, loss of autonomy, weakness and passivity of the ego, together with the various neurotic symptoms which result from this fragmentation. Kierkegaard—who wrote the only known book before Freud specifically devoted to the problem of anxiety—analyzes not only anxiety but particularly the depression and despair which result from the individual's self-estrangement, an estrangement he proceeds to classify in its different forms and degrees of severity. Nietzsche proclaims, ten years before Freud's first book, that the disease of contemporary man is that "his soul had gone stale," he is "fed up," and that all about there is a "bad smell . . . the smell of failure. . . . The leveling and diminution of European man is our greatest danger." He then proceeds to describe, in terms which remarkably predict the later psychoanalytic concepts, how blocked instinctual powers turn within the individual into resentment, self-hatred, hostility, and aggression. Freud did not know Kierkegaard's work, but he regarded Nietzsche as one of the authentically great men of all time.

What is the relation between these three giants of the nineteenth century, none of whom directly influenced either of the others? And what is the relation between the two approaches to human nature they originated—existentialism and psychoanalysis—probably the two most important to have shaken, and indeed toppled, the traditional concepts of man? To answer these questions we must inquire into the cultural situation of the middle and late nineteenth century out of which both approaches to man arose and to which both sought to give answers. The real meaning of a way of understanding human beings, such as existentialism or psychoanalysis, can never be seen *in abstracto*, detached from its world, but only in the context of the historical situation which gave it birth. Thus the historical discussions to follow in this chapter are not at all detours from our central aim. Indeed, it is precisely this historical approach which may throw light on our chief question, namely, how the specific scientific techniques that Freud developed for the investigation of the fragmentation of the individual in the Victorian period are related to the understanding of man and his crises to which Kierkegaard and Nietzsche contributed so much and which later provided a broad and deep base for existential psychotherapy.

The chief characteristic of the last half of the nineteenth century was the breaking up of personality into fragments. These fragmentations, as we shall see, were symptoms of the emotional, psychological, and spiritual disintegration occurring in the culture and in the individual. One can see this splitting up of the individual personality not only in the psychology and the science of the period but in almost every aspect of late nineteenth-century culture. One can observe the fragmentation in family life, vividly portrayed and attacked in Ibsen's *A Doll's House.* The respectable citizen who keeps his wife and family in one compartment and his business and other worlds in others is making his home a doll's house and preparing its collapse. One can likewise see the compartmentalization in the separation of art from the realities of life, the use of art in its prettified, romantic, academic forms as a hypocritical escape from existence and nature, the art as *artificiality* against which Cezanne, Van Gogh, the impressionists, and other modern art movements so vigorously protested. One can furthermore see the fragmentation in the separating of religion from weekday existence, making it an affair of Sundays and special observances, and the divorce of ethics from business. The segmentation was occurring also in philosophy and psychology—when Kierkegaard fought so passionately against the enthronement of an arid, abstract reason and pleaded for a return to reality, he was by no means tilting at windmills. The Victorian man saw himself as segmented into reason, will, and emotions and found the picture good. His reason was supposed to tell him *what* to do, then voluntaristic will was supposed to give him the means to do it, and emotions—well, emotions could best be channeled into compulsive business drive and rigidly structuralized in Victorian mores; and the emotions which would really have upset the formal segmentation, such as sex and hostility, were to be stanchly repressed or let out only in orgies of patriotism or on well-contained week-end "binges" in Bohemia in order that one might, like a steam engine which has let off surplus pressure, work more effectively on returning to his desk Monday morning. Naturally, this kind of man had to put great stress on "rationality." Indeed, the very term "irrational" means a thing not to be spoken of or thought of; and Victorian man's repressing, or compartmentalizing, what was not to be thought of was a precondition for the apparent stability of the culture. . . .

This compartmentalization went hand in hand with the developing industrialism, as both cause and effect. A man who can keep the different segments of his life entirely separated, who can punch the clock every day at exactly the same moment, whose actions are always predictable, who is never troubled by irrational urges or poetic visions, who indeed can manipulate himself the same way he would the machine whose levers he pulls, is of course the most profitable worker not only on the assembly line but even on many of the higher levels of production. As Marx and Nietzsche pointed out, the corollary is likewise true: the very success of the industrial system, with its accumulation of money as a validation of personal worth entirely separate from the actual product of a man's hands, had a reciprocal depersonalizing and dehumanizing effect upon man in his relation to others and himself. It was against these dehumanizing tendencies to make man into a machine, to make him over in the image of the industrial system for which he labored, that the early existentialists fought so strongly. And they were aware that the most serious threat of all was that reason would join mechanics in sapping the individual's vitality and decisiveness. *Reason,* they predicted, *was becoming reduced to a new kind of technique.*

Scientists in our day are often not aware that this compartmentalization, finally, was also characteristic of the sciences of the century of which we are heirs. This nineteenth century was the era of the "autonomous sciences," as Ernst Cassirer phrases it. Each science developed in its own direction; there was no unifying principle, particularly with relation to man. The views of man in the period were supported by empirical evidence amassed by the advancing sciences, but "each theory became a Procrustean bed on which the empirical facts were stretched to fit a preconceived pattern. . . . Owing to this development our modern theory of man lost its intellectual center. We acquired instead a complete anarchy of thought. . . . Theologians, scientists, politicians, sociologists, biologists, psychologists, ethnologists,

economists all approached the problem from their own viewpoints . . .
every author seems in the last count to be led by his own conception
and evaluation of human life." It is no wonder that Max Scheler
declared, "In no other period of human knowledge has man ever become more problematic to himself than in our own days. We have a
scientific, a philosophical, and a theological anthropology that know
nothing of each other. Therefore we no longer possess any clear and
consistent idea of man. The ever-growing multiplicity of the particular
sciences that are engaged in the study of men has much more confused
and obscured than elucidated our concept of man."

On the surface, of course, the Victorian period appeared placid,
contented, ordered; but this placidity was purchased at the price of
widespread, profound, and increasingly brittle repression. As in the
case of an individual neurotic, the compartmentalization became more
and more rigid as it approached the point—August 1, 1914—when it was
to collapse altogether.

Now it is to be noted that the compartmentalization of the culture
had its *psychological parallel in radical repression within the individual
personality.* Freud's genius was in developing scientific techniques for
understanding, and mayhap curing, this fragmentized individual personality; but he did not see—or until much later, when he reacted to
the fact with pessimism and some detached despair—that the neurotic
illness in the individual was only one side of disintegrating forces which
affected the whole of society. Kierkegaard, for his part, foresaw the
results of this disintegration upon the inner emotional and spiritual
life of the individual: endemic anxiety, loneliness, estrangement of
one man from another, and finally the condition that would lead to
ultimate despair, man's alienation from himself. But it remained for
Nietzsche to paint most graphically the approaching situation: "We
live in a period of atoms, of atomic chaos," and out of this chaos he
foresaw, in a vivid prediction of collectivism in the twentieth century,
"the terrible apparition . . . the Nation State . . . and the hunt for
happiness will never be greater than when 'it must be caught between
today and tomorrow; because the day after tomorrow all hunting time
may have come to an end altogether. . . ." Freud saw this fragmentation of personality in the light of natural science and was concerned
with formulating its technical aspects. Kierkegaard and Nietzsche did
not underestimate the importance of the specific psychological analysis;
but they were much more concerned with understanding *man as the
being who represses,* the being who surrenders self-awareness as a

protection against reality and then suffers the neurotic consequences. The strange question is: What does it mean that man, the being-in-the-world who can be conscious that he exists and can know his existence, should choose or be forced to choose to block off this consciousness and should suffer anxiety, compulsions for self-destruction, and despair? Kierkegaard and Nietzsche were keenly aware that the "sickness of the soul" of Western man was a deeper and more extensive morbidity than could be explained by the specific individual or social problems. Something was radically wrong in man's relation to himself; man had become fundamentally problematic to himself. "This is Europe's true predicament," declared Nietzche; "together with the fear of man we have lost the love of man, confidence in man, indeed, *the will to man.*" . . .

We now come to a very important problem, and in order to understand it we need to make one more preliminary distinction. That is between "reason" as the term was used in the seventeenth century and the enlightenment and "technical reason" today. Freud held a concept of reason which came directly from the enlightenment, namely, "ecstatic reason." And he equated this with science. This use of reason involves, as seen in Spinoza and the other thinkers of the seventeenth and eighteenth centuries, a confidence that reason can by itself comprehend all problems. But those thinkers were using reason as including the capacity to transcend the immediate situation, to grasp the whole, and such functions as intuition, insight, poetic perception were not rigidly excluded. The concept also embraced ethics: reason in the enlightenment meant justice. Much, in other words, that is "irrational" was included in their idea of reason. This accounts for the tremendous and enthusiastic faith they could lodge in it. But by the end of the nineteenth century, as Tillich demonstrates most cogently, this ecstatic character had been lost. Reason had become "technical reason": reason married to techniques, reason as functioning best when devoted to isolated problems, reason as an adjunct and subordinate to technical industrial progress, reason as separated off from emotion and will, reason indeed as opposed to existence—the reason finally which Kierkegaard and Nietzsche so strongly attacked.

Now, part of the time Freud uses the concept of reason in the ecstatic form, as when he speaks of reason as "our salvation," reason as our "only recourse," and so on. Here one gets the anachronistic feeling that his sentences are directly out of Spinoza or some writer of the enlightenment. Thus he tried on one hand to preserve the ecstatic concept, tried to save the view of man and reason which transcends techniques. But, on the other hand, in equating reason with science, Freud makes it technical reason. His great contribution was his effort to overcome the fragmentation of man by bringing man's irrational tendencies into the light, bringing unconscious, split off, and repressed aspects of personality into consciousness and acceptance. But the other side of his emphasis, namely, the identification of psychoanalysis with technical reason, is an expression of the precise fragmentation which he sought to cure. It is not unfair to say that the prevailing trend in the development of psychoanalysis in late decades, particularly after the death of Freud, has been to reject his efforts to save reason in its ecstatic form and to accept exclusively the latter—namely, reason in its technical form. This trend is generally unnoticed, since it fits in so well with dominant trends in our whole culture. But we have already noted that seeing man and his functions in their technical form is one of the central factors in the compartmentalization of contemporary man. Thus a critical and serious dilemma faces us. On the theoretical side, psychoanalysis (and other forms of psychology to the extent that they are wedded to technical reason) themselves add to the chaos in our theory of man, both scientific and philosophical, of which Cassirer and Scheler spoke above. On the practical side, there is considerable danger that psychoanalysis, as well as other forms of psychotherapy and adjustment psychology, will become new representations of the fragmentation of man, that they will exemplify the loss of the individual's vitality and significance, rather than the reverse, that the new techniques will assist in standardizing and giving cultural sanction to man's alienation from himself rather than solving it, that they will become expressions of the new mechanization of man, now calculated and controlled with greater psychological precision and on the vaster scale of unconscious and depth dimensions—that psychoanalysis and psychotherapy in general will become part of the neurosis of our day rather than part of the cure. This would indeed be a supreme irony of history. It is not alarmism nor showing unseemly fervor to point out these tendencies, some of which are already upon us; it is simply to look directly at our historical situation and to draw unflinchingly the implications.

We are now in a position to see the crucial significance of the existential psychotherapy movement. It is precisely the movement that protests against the tendency to identify psychotherapy with technical reason. It stands for basing psychotherapy on an understanding of what makes man the *human* being; it stands for defining neurosis in terms of what destroys man's capacity to fulfill his own being. We have seen that Kierkegaard and Nietzsche, as well as the representatives of the existential cultural movement following them, not only contributed far-reaching and penetrating psychological insights, which in themselves form a significant contribution to anyone seeking scientifically to understand modern psychological problems, but also did something else—they placed these insights on an ontological basis, namely, the study of *man as the being who has* these particular problems. They believed that it was absolutely necessary that this be done, and they feared that the subordination of reason to technical problems would ultimately mean the making of man over in the image of the machine. Science, Nietzsche had warned, is becoming a factory, and the result will be ethical nihilism.

Existential psychotherapy is the movement which, although standing on one side on the scientific analysis owed chiefly to the genius of Freud, also brings back into the picture the understanding of man on the deeper and broader level—man as the being who is human. It is based on the assumption that it is possible to have a science of man which does not fragmentize man and destroy his humanity at the same moment as it studies him. It unites science and ontology. . . .